1982

Preface Books

A series of scholarly and critical studies of major writers intended for those needing modern and authoritative guidance through the characteristic difficulties of their work to reach an intelligent understanding and enjoyment of it.

General Editor: MAURICE HUSSEY

Available now :

A Preface to Wordsworth	JOHN PURKIS
A Preface to Donne	JAMES WINNY
A Preface to Milton	LOIS POTTER
A Preface to Coleridge	ALLAN GRANT
A Preface to Jane Austen	CHRISTOPHER GILLIE
A Preface to Yeats	EDWARD MALINS
A Preface to Pope	I.R.F. GORDON
A Preface to Hardy	MERRYN WILLIAMS
A Preface to Dryden	DAVID WYKES
A Preface to Spenser	HELENA SHIRE
A Preface to James Joyce	SYDNEY BOLT
A Preface to Hopkins	GRAHAM STOREY

Titles in preparation :

A Preface to Conrad	CEDRIC WATTS
A Preface to Lawrence	GĀMINI SALGĀDO
A Preface to Forster	CHRISTOPHER GILLIE

A Preface to Hopkins

Graham Storey

Longman London and New York

LONGMAN GROUP LIMITED
Longman House
Burnt Mill, Harlow, Essex CM20 2JE, England

Published in the United States of America
by Longman Inc., New York

First published 1981

British Library Cataloguing in Publication Data
Storey, Graham
    A preface to Hopkins.—(Preface books).
    1. Hopkins, Gerard Manley—Criticism and interpretation
    I. Title   II. Series
    821'.8   PR4803.H44Z/   79-41680

ISBN 0 582 35251 7 cased
    0 582 35252 5 paper

Set in 10/11 pt Monophoto Baskerville
by Pearl Island Filmsetters (HK) Ltd.
Printed in Hong Kong by
Wing Tai Cheung Printing Co. Ltd.

To the memory of my mother and father,
Winifred and Stanley Storey.

GRAHAM STOREY completed *The Journals and Papers of G.M. Hopkins* (1959), after the death of their first editor, Humphry House. He edited *Hopkins: Selections* (poems and selected prose, 1967), and has lectured on Hopkins in Eastern Europe and Japan. He is also joint General Editor of the Pilgrim edition of *Dickens's Letters*. He is a Fellow of Trinity Hall, Cambridge, and a University Lecturer in English.

Contents

List of illustrations

Foreword

The sympathetic conception and lucid execution that distinguish the biographical section of this book by Graham Storey readily draw the reader into the perceptive account of the ideas and poetry of the isolated Jesuit, Gerard Manley Hopkins, which are the crown of the whole undertaking. Any study of Hopkins must express the oddity of the rhythm, sound and syntax in which he worked and the way in which he was both a Victorian and yet also a peer of the modernists and expressionists into whose world he came by chance as a result of publication denied and then much delayed. One sees in his predicament the advantage of working in isolation without a thought of immediate publication: the rapid change from a rhapsodic nature poetry in the manner of John Keats to a forceful and intense self-scrutiny couched in language more original than any found in English since the renaissance. The disadvantages were that his necessary audience consisted of three traditionally-minded fellow poets during his lifetime and, once publication had been effected in 1918, a still small and largely uncomprehending segment of a poetry-reading public hardly ready for it. The harvest came in the 1930s, when at last Hopkins was recognized as the most distinguished religious poet since John Donne and George Herbert, the latter a forerunner he particularly admired.

Mr Storey, a Hopkins scholar of international repute who has worked closely with the poetry and the prose for a considerable time, is able to support the reader at every point throughout his deeply considered and lucid study. It is a welcome addition to a series notable for the insight and distinction of its authors.

This volume appears, incidentally, with a jacket-illustration that was an inevitable choice for the author and myself. To me it is not only the celebrated windhover, discussed on pages 104 to 107, but a symbol of the poet who was also a painter of note and possessed a hawk's eye for the shimmering of trees, flowers, clouds and waves. From his intricate study of philosophy and theology and the entire Jesuit aesthetic he understood it his duty to reveal the sacramental presence of the creator throughout the universe. It was, he knew, his task to recreate all this and that nothing short of total originality of poetic technique could accomplish it. For those who are defeated by some of the details but sense the communion that Hopkins intended with his readers the present book has much wisdom to offer.

MAURICE HUSSEY
General Editor

Introduction

Hopkins is unique among major English poets in being virtually unknown until forty years after his death. The first full edition of his poems (750 copies only), edited by Robert Bridges in 1918, took twelve years to sell. Bridges's *Preface* made it abundantly clear that Hopkins could never have been a major Victorian or even Georgian poet. But he has been hailed emphatically as a major poet by this century, and each new generation of readers of poetry continues to be moved and excited by him.

Many of Hopkins's poetic qualities are traditional: his remarkable rhythmic skill, his superb gift of image-making, the energy and expressiveness of his language. But he is also one of our greatest experimental poets: an innovator in language, in using the resources of words to the utmost; in rhythm, in creating patterns of sound and stress that—to use his own phrase—'fetch out' the meaning; in syntax, in jettisoning, wherever he can, every word that does not tell. These experiments bring with them linguistic difficulties: nevertheless—or perhaps because of the challenge involved—they appeal strongly to the twentieth-century reader. But we are moved and impressed just as much, I think, by Hopkins's strongly individual qualities of temperament and character: by his honesty, his candour, his precision; by his exactitude and self-exactingness in expressing his solitary experience. These qualities demand as much courage as his more famous technical innovations; and in Hopkins the two go together. Few poets other than Shakespeare have Hopkins's power of expressing the mysterious extremes of feeling: both the exciting 'otherness' of natural power and beauty and the terrifying 'otherness' of despair. And probably no poet has expressed so convincingly the mystery of selfhood: what, in one of his finest prose passages, he called 'that taste of myself, of *I* and *me* above and in all things, which is more distinctive than the taste of ale or alum, more distinctive than the smell of walnut leaf or camphor, and is incommunicable by any means to another man'.

For Hopkins, his poetry had to be religious. It either praised God through His creations or charted Hopkins's own despair when he felt deserted by God. Yet for us it crosses normal religious barriers. He is the greatest modern English religious poet; but his admirers include a vast number of agnostics. Hopkins once wrote of Wordsworth's *Ode on Intimations of Immortality* that, in contemplating it, human nature—as in contemplating Plato—'got a shock', and 'the tremble from it is spreading'. I am, he said, 'ever since I knew the ode, in that tremble'. It is a state understood and shared by many lovers of Hopkins's own poetry.

Part One
The Poet in his Setting

The Hopkins and Smith families

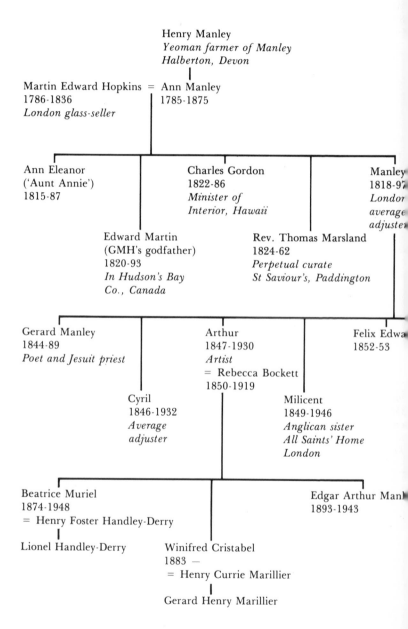

Henry Manley
*Yeoman farmer of Manley
Halberton, Devon*

Martin Edward Hopkins = Ann Manley
1786-1836   1785-1875
London glass-seller

Ann Eleanor
('Aunt Annie')
1815-87

Charles Gordon
1822-86
*Minister of
Interior, Hawaii*

Manley
1818-97
*London
average
adjuster*

Edward Martin
(GMH's godfather)
1820-93
*In Hudson's Bay
Co., Canada*

Rev. Thomas Marsland
1824-62
*Perpetual curate
St Saviour's, Paddington*

Gerard Manley
1844-89
Poet and Jesuit priest

Arthur
1847-1930
Artist
= Rebecca Bockett
1850-1919

Felix Edwa
1852-53

Cyril
1846-1932
*Average
adjuster*

Milicent
1849-1946
*Anglican sister
All Saints' Home
London*

Beatrice Muriel
1874-1948
= Henry Foster Handley-Derry

Edgar Arthur Man
1893-1943

Lionel Handley-Derry

Winifred Cristabel
1883 —
= Henry Currie Marillier

Gerard Henry Marillier

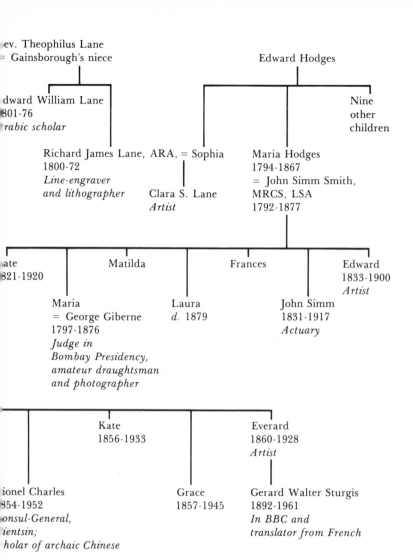

ev. Theophilus Lane
= Gainsborough's niece

Edward Hodges

dward William Lane
801-76
rabic scholar

Nine
other
children

Richard James Lane, ARA, = Sophia
1800-72
*Line-engraver
and lithographer*

Clara S. Lane
Artist

Maria Hodges
1794-1867
= John Simm Smith,
MRCS, LSA
1792-1877

ate
821-1920

Matilda

Frances

Edward
1833-1900
Artist

Maria
= George Giberne
1797-1876
*Judge in
Bombay Presidency,
amateur draughtsman
and photographer*

Laura
d. 1879

John Simm
1831-1917
Actuary

Kate
1856-1933

Everard
1860-1928
Artist

ionel Charles
854-1952
*onsul-General,
ientsin;
holar of archaic Chinese*

Grace
1857-1945

Gerard Walter Sturgis
1892-1961
*In BBC and
translator from French*

ESSE QUAM VIDERI

3

Chronological table

	HOPKINS'S LIFE	LITERARY AND HISTORICAL EVENTS
1844	Born at Stratford, Essex (28 July).	
1845		Newman received into the Roman Catholic Church.
1852	Family moves to Oak Hill, Hampstead. At a day-school in Hampstead.	
1854	Boarder at Highgate School.	
1857	Tour through Belgium and the Rhineland with his father and brother.	
1859		Darwin's *Origin of Species*.
1860	Wins school poetry prize with *The Escorial* (Easter). Tour through south Germany with his father.	*Essays and Reviews* published.
1863	*Winter with the Gulf Stream* published in *Once a Week*, 14 February. Wins a Classical Exhibition to Balliol College, Oxford.	
1863–7	At Balliol College. Meets Robert Bridges, Alexander Baillie, William Addis. Writes most of his early poetry; sketches a good deal.	
1864	Takes a First in 'Mods'.	

1865	Meets Digby Mackworth Dolben (February). Has religious crisis and begins his daily spiritual notes (March).	
1866	Decides to leave the Church of England (17 or 18 July). Received into the Roman Catholic Church by Newman at the Birmingham Oratory (21 October).	Swinburne's *Poems and Ballads*.
1867	Takes a First in 'Greats' and graduates B.A. In Paris (July).	
1867–8	Teaches at the Oratory School, Birmingham.	
1868	Decides to become a priest and a Jesuit. Burns his early poems (11 May). Walking-tour in Switzerland with Edward Bond (July). Enters the Jesuit Novitiate, Roehampton (7 September).	
1869		Matthew Arnold's *Culture and Anarchy*.
1870		Franco-Prussian War.
1870–3	Studies Philosophy at St Mary's Hall, Stonyhurst.	
1873–4	Teaches 'Rhetoric' at Roehampton, including a course on 'Poetry and verse'.	
1874–7	Studies Theology at St Bueno's College, North Wales.	

1875–6 Writes *The Wreck of the Deutschland* (December–January).

1877 Ordained priest (23 September).

1877–8 Sub-minister at Mount St Mary's College, Chesterfield.

1878 Select Preacher at Farm Street Church, London (August). Correspondence with R.W. Dixon begins (June).

1878–9 Priest at St Aloysius's Church, Oxford.

1879 On temporary staff at St Joseph's, Bedford Leigh, near Manchester (October).

1880–1 Priest at St Francis Xavier's, Liverpool.

1881 On temporary staff at St Joseph's, Glasgow (August–October).

1881–2 'Tertianship' at Roehampton.

1882–4 Teaches Classics at Stonyhurst College.

1882   Murder of Lord Frederick Cavendish and Thomas Burke in Phoenix Park, Dublin.

1883 Correspondence with Coventry Patmore begins (August). In Holland with his parents (August).

1884–9	Professor of Greek, University College, Dublin, and Fellow of the Royal University.	
1886		Alliance of Gladstone and Parnell for Irish Home Rule. First Home Rule Bill defeated.
1889	Dies in Dublin of typhoid fever (8 June). Buried in Glasnevin Cemetery, Dublin.	
1893	Eleven of his poems (three of them extracts) published by Robert Bridges in A.H. Milne's *Poets and Poetry of the Century*.	
1915	Six of his poems (two of them extracts) published by Robert Bridges in *The Spirit of Man*.	
1918	*Poems of Gerard Manley Hopkins* published, edited by Robert Bridges.	

1 Hopkins's life

Family background and school

The Hopkins family was prosperous, cultivated and, on both sides, had connections with the fine arts. Hopkins's great-uncle on his mother's side, Richard Lane, was Gainsborough's great-nephew and himself a distinguished line-engraver and lithographer who exhibited regularly at the Royal Academy. His uncle, again on his mother's side, Edward Smith, was a professional watercolour painter. Two of his father's brothers married granddaughters of the portrait painter, Sir William Beechey; and one of them, Frances Ann Hopkins, whose husband was in the Hudson's Bay Company, became well known in Canada as a painter of *voyageurs*, the canoemen in the fur trade. Other relations were minor artists.

When Gerard was born, on 28 July 1844, the eldest of three sisters and five brothers, his parents, who had married a year before, were living in Stratford, Essex. His father, Manley Hopkins, was clearly something of a dilettante, but achieved a fair measure of success in his remarkably diverse interests. He ran his own marine insurance firm in the City; was Consul-General for Hawaii in London for forty years; and published a variety of books, including three volumes of verse. The Hawaiian connection must have brought an unexpectedly exotic element into the Hopkins home.

Gerard's mother, Catherine Hopkins (*née* Simm Smith), was the daughter of a successful London doctor. She greatly valued her son's poems and lived to see them published in 1918, when she was ninety-seven. Soon after Gerard's birth, her father moved from London to Blunt House, Croydon, a large house in what was then the country. Gerard certainly spent periods of his boyhood there (his youngest brother Lionel described it as 'a second home'); and an early drawing, done when he was eighteen, is of weeds ('Dandelion, Hemlock and Ivy') in one of its fields.

As in so many Victorian homes, an unmarried aunt lived with the family and played a large part in educating the children: Manley's sister Ann Eleanor Hopkins, 'Aunt Annie', a talented amateur painter, who encouraged Gerard's early drawing and music. In 1864 he described her in a letter as 'deep in archaeology etc. etc.'. She clearly fostered similar talents in some of the other children too. Two of Gerard's brothers, Arthur and Everard, became well-known artists and illustrators; and one sister, Katie, had a marked gift for drawing. Several of Arthur's sketchbook drawings, reproduced in *All My Eyes See: the visual world of G.M. Hopkins*, show a strong

Hopkins, aged 14½, by Ann Eleanor Hopkins

Hopkins's father,
Manley Hopkins,
October 1876

Hopkins's mother,
Catherine Hopkins

affinity with Gerard's early sketches. Another sister, Grace, was an accomplished musician and later set accompaniments to Gerard's melodies for poems by Bridges and R.W. Dixon. His eldest sister, Milicent, became an Anglican nun. Perhaps the most interesting of Gerard's brothers, for the way in which he used linguistic talents in a way quite different to Gerard's, was the youngest, Lionel, who, after a career in the British Consular Service in China, retired early and became a scholar of worldwide reputation of the Chinese language. The last survivor of the family, he died in 1952, aged ninety-seven. He greatly admired Gerard, and the one letter from Gerard to him that has survived shows the philological interests they had in common.

The Hopkins family was clearly a closely-knit and affectionate one, with strongly shared interests in poetry, painting, music and word-play. It is disappointing that no letters or comments which might have illuminated Gerard's relations with his mother and father, or with any of his brothers and sisters, seem to have survived before he went up to Oxford.

In 1852 the family moved to Oak Hill, Hampstead, where they stayed for thirty-four years. For two years Gerard went to a day-school in Hampstead. Then in September 1854 he moved to Highgate School (originally Sir Roger Cholmeley's Grammar School, by then a small public school). For most of his eight years there he was a day-boy, then finally a boarder in Elgin House. His headmaster was the Rev. John Bradley Dyne, D.D., former Dean of Wadham College, Oxford: a good teacher of the Classics (the study of which, according to Edmund Yates, who was at Highgate a few years before Gerard, he considered 'the primary object of our creation'); but, as a head-master, heavy-handed and tyrannical (the 'Patriarch of the Old Dispensation' Gerard called him). It was probably inevitable that a boy as intellectually precocious, sensitive and sharply individual as Gerard should clash with such a man—particularly if he felt a sense of injustice. But a letter he wrote in his final year to his friend Charles Luxmoore, who had just left, reads amazingly—even for 1862: 'Dyne and I had a terrific altercation. I was driven out of patience and cheeked him wildly, and he blazed into me with his riding-whip.' After 'a worse row' in which his co-victim 'was flogged, struck off the confirmation list and fined £1', Gerard was 'deprived of [his] room for ever, sent to bed at half past nine till further orders, and ordered to work *only* in the school room, not even in the school library'. After a final misdemeanour, 'Dyne . . . sent me to bed at nine and for the third time this quarter threatened expulsion, de-privation'. This harsh treatment seems all the stranger when we read the impressions of Gerard by his younger brother Cyril, who followed him to Highgate and later compared him to the young Swinburne:

There is a passage in Lord Redesdale's *Memoirs* relating to the school-days of Swinburne, so suitable to those of my brother Gerard that I cannot resist quoting it: 'Of games he took no heed —they were not for his frail build; football and cricket were nothing to him. And so he led a sort of charmed life, dreaming and reading, and chewing the cud of his gleanings from the world-harvest of poetry, a fairy child in the midst of a commonplace, workaday world.' And like Swinburne, he was not deficient either in moral or in physical courage, for he was a fearless climber of trees, and would go up very high in the lofty elm tree, standing in our garden . . . to the alarm of onlookers like myself.

Any resemblance to Swinburne ends there. In the *Poetry Review*, 1942, Lancelot de Giberne Sieveking told stories of Gerard's visits to the Giberne family home at Epsom as a boy: of his intent listening to bird song, and his 'arranging stones and twigs in rows and patterns, with infinite care' (anticipating an old lay brother's memories of him at Stonyhurst in 1882, recorded by Denis Meadows in 1913: 'Ay, a strange young man, crouching down that gate to stare at some wet sand. A fair natural 'e seemed to us, that Mr 'opkins.') Mr Sieveking's stories came from his mother, Gerard's cousin; his grandfather was Gerard's uncle, George Giberne, retired Chief Judge of the East India Company, and a very early photographer.

Despite his rows with the headmaster, Gerard had an exemplary school career. He won several prizes for Classics, a gold medal for Latin verse, a school scholarship, and in 1863 an Exhibition to Balliol College, Oxford. By then he had also won a school prize for his poem, *The Escorial*, written when he was only fifteen; and also written *A Vision of the Mermaids* (illustrated with a pen-and-ink drawing, reproduced opposite) and *Winter with the Gulf Stream*. This was published in *Once a Week*, on 14 February 1863, when he was eighteen—almost his only poem to be published in his lifetime. And whatever his relations with the headmaster, he was popular with his schoolfellows. They found him likable if eccentric; but both sensitive and strong-willed to an unusual degree. The poet R.W. Dixon, who spent a few months in 1861 as a master at Highgate and later became a friend and important correspondent of Gerard's, wrote to him in 1878 that he remembered him clearly as 'a pale young boy, very light and active, with a very meditative and intellectual face'. His appearance, and his nickname of 'Skin', probably belied the strength of his will, already exercised on one occasion at least on self-denial. Both his brother Cyril and Charles Luxmoore tell the story of how, for a bet—the real reason being 'a conversation on seamen's sufferings and human powers of endurance'—he abstained from all liquids for a week (Luxmoore says, impossibly,

A Vision of the Mermaids

Rowing, I reach'd a rock – the sea was low –
Which the tides cover in their overflow,
Marking the spot, when they have gurgled o'er,
With a thin floating veil of water hoar.
A mile astern lay the blue shores away;
And it was at the setting of the day.

  Plum-purple was the west; but spikes of
                          light
Spear'd open lustrous gashes, crimson-white;
(Where the eye fix'd, fled the encrimsoning
                  spot,   [was not;)
And gathering, floated where the gaze
And thro' their parting lids there came and
                          went
Keen glimpses of the inner firmament:
Fair beds they seem'd of water-lily flakes
Clustering entrancingly in beryl lakes:
Anon, across their swimming splendour
                          strook,   [shook
An intense line of throbbing blood-light
A quivering pennon; then, for eye too keen,

Ebb'd back beneath its snowy lids, unseen.
Now all things rosy turn'd: the west
                  had grown   [blown
To an orb'd rose, which, by hot pantings
Apart, betwixt ten thousand petall'd lips
By interchange gasp'd splendour and e-
                          clipse.
The zenith melted to a rose of air; [glare
The waves were rosy-lipp'd; the crimson
Shower'd the cliffs and every fret and
                          spire [-budded bine.
With garnet wreaths and blooms of rosy-
  Then, looking on the waters, I was ware
Of something drifting thro' delighted air,
—An isle of roses,—and another near;—
And more, on each hand, thicken, and
                          appear
In shoals of bloom; as in unpeopled skies,
Save by two stars, more crowding lights a-
                          rise, [mazed eyes.
And planets bud wheree'er we turn our

Part of the first page of Hopkins's A Vision of the Mermaids

13

Rock in the cliff copse, Shanklin. Sketch by Hopkins.

for three weeks). Gerard won the bet, but collapsed at drill with a blackened tongue, and was immediately punished by Dyne.

One of his closer school-friends was Ernest Hartley Coleridge, grandson of the poet, with whom, in one long letter, Gerard discusses Theocritus, Aeschylus and Tennyson, and sends long fragments of three more of his own poems. Another was Marcus Clarke (the 'co-victim' above), who achieved some fame as a writer in Australia, particularly with his convict novel *For the Term of his Natural Life*. Clarke greatly admired Gerard, putting him into at least two of his stories; in return, Clarke was a recipient of Gerard's early fascination with words: 'Marcus Scrivener,' he called him, 'a kaleidoscopic, parti-coloured, harlequinesque, thaumotropic being.'

This sense of fun was one of the things that Charles Luxmoore most remembered in him: 'He was full of fun, rippling over with

Shanklin, Isle of Wight. Sketch by Hopkins.

jokes, and chaff, facile with pencil and pen, with rhyming jibe or cartoon.' It comes out strongly in some of the charming, lighthearted drawings of his schooldays that have survived. It alternates too with one brief reference showing the seriousness with which he treated his friendships (and the pain they could cause him), which he quoted to Luxmoore from a Journal he kept for 1862 (parts of which he later burnt).

But his drawing was much more than fun. G.F. Lahey, S.J., writing about Gerard's boyhood, no doubt had evidence to state that, had Gerard not decided to become a Catholic priest, 'he would undoubtedly have adopted painting for his profession, as a future drawing-master strongly advised him to do'. (*G.M. Hopkins*, 1930, p. 2). After his first year at Oxford, Gerard wrote to his undergraduate friend Alexander Baillie: 'I have now a more rational hope than before of doing something—in poetry and painting. . . . about the latter . . . I have great things to tell.' And, after he had decided to take orders, four years later, he wrote to Baillie again: 'You know I once wanted to be a painter.'

Gerard made two early visits to the Continent with his father: to Belgium and the Rhineland when he was thirteen, and to southern Germany at sixteen. From Nuremberg, says Lahey, he enclosed 'some first-rate sketches of Bavarian peasantry'. His surviving drawings date from 1862, two years later; the most impressive of them a group of seven pencil sketches done on a family holiday in the Isle of Wight in July–August 1863 (his first long vacation from Oxford). They are of rocks, waves, clouds, trees and—perhaps the best-known—an iris; apart from their merit as remarkably fresh and beautifully observed drawings, they have a particular interest: for in their intense apprehension of nature they clearly anticipate the 'inscapes' (his own later coined word for a thing's distinctive, inner form) that both his Journal (kept from 1866 to 1875) and, ultimately, his mature poems aimed to express. More drawings illustrate his Journal —the most ambitious ones done on a Swiss tour of 1868, a few months before he entered the Jesuit novitiate. And many years later, in 1884, he wrote to his sister Kate, regretting that he had given up his drawing:

> A dear old French Father . . . finding that once I used to draw, got me to bring him the few remains I still have, cows and horses in chalk done in Wales too long ago to think of, and admired them to that degree that he is urgent with me to go on drawing at all hazards; but I do not see how that could be now, so late: if any-body had said the same 10 years ago it might have been different.

Hopkins's last two terms at school witness a new excitement in writing. 'I have been writing numbers of descriptions of sunrises, sunsets, sunlight in the trees, flowers, windy skies etc. etc.', he told E.H. Coleridge, in a letter sending him three long fragments of poems.

> I have begun the story of the Corinthian capital; of course you know it; I think we spoke of it before. I have done two thirds of 'Linnington Water, an Idyll', and am planning 'Fause Joan' a ballad in the old style. All these things are done in scraps of time.

His love of the Classics remained, indeed grew stronger. But he had clearly outgrown Highgate and its restrictions. 'The truth is I had no love for my schooldays and wished to banish the remem-brance of them', he wrote years later to his friend Canon Dixon. Oxford was to be very different. He went up to Balliol College to read Classics in April 1863 and thrived from the start. 'Not to love my University would be to undo the very buttons of my being', he wrote to Baillie seventeen years later.

The Balliol that Hopkins went up to in April 1863 was a small college of less than a hundred undergraduates, but a very distinguished one. After a long period of intellectual lethargy that had afflicted most of Oxford, Balliol had been one of the first colleges in the 1830s to reform itself, to set high standards of scholarship and intellectual enquiry; and, above all, of dedicated teaching. Most of the undergraduates, like Hopkins himself, read Classics—*Literae Humaniores* ('Greats'), as the Honours school is called at Oxford—: Greek and Latin language and literature, ancient history and philosophy; and, academically, the 1860s were probably Balliol's most impressive decade. In the four years that Hopkins was up, Balliol men gained nearly a quarter of the first class degrees in Classics awarded throughout the University. Hopkins shared in this impressive achievement by taking firsts himself, as he was expected to, in both Honour 'Mods' (in 1864) and 'Greats' (in 1866).

Academic success was rated highly in Balliol; and Hopkins's diaries and letters are full of delight at his friends' achievements and commiseration for the 'disasters'. He was intensely proud of his college. 'He is the cleverest man in Balliol, that is in the University, or in the University, that is in Balliol, whichever you like', he wrote to his mother about one contemporary. But Balliol was also the centre of advanced thought at Oxford, and of the religious controversy that went with it. Both were identified to an unusual degree with Benjamin Jowett, a Fellow since 1838 and far and away the most influential of the Tutors. Jowett was a legendary figure long before he became Master of Balliol in 1870; and both his supporters and detractors are agreed on the remarkable influence that he exerted. The aim he set himself as a teacher was the Socratic one: to reach the truth by questioning; to clarify, not to impart ideas; to encourage his pupils to use their own minds. He was totally dedicated and immensely hard-working: besides his college lectures and tutorials, he lectured, as University Professor of Greek (at a salary of £40 a year), on Plato's *Republic*: the beginnings of his great translation of Plato that made him famous. Hopkins was never a 'Jowett-worshipper', as Jowett's inner circle of pupils were called; but it is clear that he came under his spell. According to Hopkins's friend Martin Geldart, a Balliol contemporary, it was Jowett's 'purity' which struck Hopkins: 'what had he been but a Catholic, he would have called his "saintliness"' (*A Son of Belial*, 1882, Geldart's thinly disguised autobiography). This is the more striking, since tutor and pupil stood at opposite ends of the religious spectrum: Jowett, the acknowledged leader of the Oxford Broad Church party; Hopkins, a devout Anglo-Catholic ('my Ritualistic friend', Geldart calls him in *A Son of Belial*). Hopkins wrote essays for Jowett and was advised to take great pains with them; was embarrassed by his famous silences, but, when he could get him to talk, found him 'amusing'. Jowett, according to Jesuit sources, said later that he 'never met a more promising pupil'; Fr Lahey, Hopkins's first biographer, says that Jowett called Hopkins 'the star of Balliol'.

His other Balliol tutors and their lectures Hopkins sums up succinctly in his first letter to his mother:

> Among the other tutors are Riddell . . . he lectures on Aeschylus and Homer; he and his lectures are much thought of and popular: Woolcomb [E.C. Woollcombe], or 'Woolx', a pinch-faced old man, whom everybody likes as much as they yawn over his divinity lectures: and Oily Smith, the mathematical master, who has given me a paper in Algebra to try my powers. Palmer's lectures in Aeschines and Virgil shew a height of scholarship which makes me awestruck. When he lectures, he does not hesitate, as in private, but reads long passages into the most beautiful fluent English.

Scholarship and power of language Hopkins was always to admire. But, in a Balliol whose recent *alumni* included Matthew Arnold (now Oxford Professor of Poetry) and Arthur Hugh Clough, he equally admired moral earnestness; and, after Jowett, the tutor who probably most influenced him was Jowett's closest ally, the philosopher T.H. Green. Hopkins's first reference to him was sharp enough: 'of a rather offensive style of infidelity, and naturally dislikes the beauties of nature'. But that was after Green and another Fellow had had a beech tree in the Balliol quad cut down, something Hopkins was always to find hard to forgive. Thereafter, as his 'Greats' tutor (Green was to do distinguished work on Hegel and Kant and Hume), Hopkins liked and admired him; and Green reciprocated his feelings. As a teacher, Green was a system-builder, the opposite of Jowett. He certainly did not convert Hopkins to his own German idealism; but an extant essay by Hopkins on Plato, initialled by Green, has, as we should have expected, a strongly idealist approach.

Green was upset at Hopkins's decision to become a Jesuit and wrote to a pupil and friend who had been to see him at Roehampton:

> A step such as he has taken, tho' I can't quite admit it to be heroic, must needs be painful, and its pain should not be aggravated—as it is pretty sure to be—by separation from old friends. . . . I imagine him—perhaps uncharitably—to be one of those, like his ideal J.H. Newman, who instead of simply opening themselves to the revelation of God in the reasonable world, are fain to put themselves into an attitude—saintly, it is true, but still an attitude. . . . It vexes me to the heart to think of a fine nature being victimised

by a system which in my 'historic conscience' I hold to be sub-versive of the Family and the State, and which puts the service of an exceptional institution, or the saving of the individual soul, in opposition to loyal service to society.

Hopkins's letter to his mother, summing up his tutors, has much more to say of his friends; and for his first two years at Balliol their names crowd his diaries and letters. 'At the present rate it appears likely I shall know all Oxford in six weeks. I have not breakfasted in my own rooms for 10 days I think; (*ten* days: I am afraid you will consider the numerals vulgar.).' Breakfast parties and small wine parties, or simply inviting a friend for wine in one's rooms, were the accepted forms of Oxford entertainment; and Hopkins was clearly a sought-after guest. Another meeting-place was the Union, the Oxford debating society, which had many of the amenities of a London club: Hopkins joined it in his first term, though he did not speak in its debates. Rowing, cricket and racquets were almost the only organized sports; non-athletes like Hopkins took their exercise in long walks with friends and boating on the river. Boating gave Hopkins particular pleasure: 'I know nothing so luxuriously delicious as a canoe. . . . The motion is Elysian. . . . A canoe in the Cherwel[l] must be the summit of human happiness.' But the impression of these early letters is that almost everything Oxford offered gave Hopkins pleasure: 'Except for much work and that I can never keep my hands cool, I am almost too happy.'

Hopkins's early friends were remarkably varied in their religious backgrounds and beliefs; Martin Geldart in *A Son of Belial* stresses how much these mattered in the Balliol of the 1860s. He thus describes the 'scholars' table':

Never in all my life before or since was I among a company of men so young and ardent, yet so utterly devoted to plain living and high thinking. Never was I in an intellectual atmosphere so fearless and so free. I never knew what true tolerance without indifference was till I came to [Oxford]. It was a new experience to me altogether—to me, who had been brought up to regard Ritualism and Rationalism as the two right arms of the devil, to find myself suddenly launched among a lot of men who were some of them Ritualists of the deepest dye, some of them Rationalists, some of them Positivists, some of them Materialists, all eager in advancing their respective views, and yet all ready to listen with courtesy to their opponents.

Geldart himself was a strict Evangelical. Hopkins gave his mother a vivid caricature of his physical appearance, 'his full haggard hideousness', in his first letter to her; they then saw a lot of each other, and Hopkins stayed with his family near Manchester in July 1865.

Hopkins's closest undergraduate friend was William Addis, son of a Free Church Minister of Edinburgh, one of what he called 'the High-Church section at Balliol'. Many years after Hopkins's death, Addis wrote: 'I knew him in his undergraduate days far better than any one else did. ... We walked together almost daily. ... I re-member long arguments we had on the eternity of punishment ... ' Hopkins and he shared lodgings in Oxford in 1866 and went on a walking-tour together that June. Addis became a Roman Catholic just before Hopkins, and a priest in 1872. After sixteen years he renounced the Catholic Church (much to Hopkins's pain) and married; after a period as a Presbyterian Minister and then as a Unitarian, he returned to the Church of England and spent his last ten years as an Anglican priest. Few of Hopkins's friends had quite such unusual careers.

A lifelong friend made at Balliol was Alexander Baillie, son of an Edinburgh doctor. After taking first classes in 'Mods' and 'Greats', as had Addis, he was called to the Bar and practised in Lincoln's Inn. Brought up a Presbyterian, he was a strong rationalist; and his rationalism, according to an account by a friend's daughter, 'made a kind of atheist of him'. But there is no evidence that his scepticism put Hopkins off. Rather the reverse: Hopkins's early letters to Baillie are some of the best that he wrote: affectionate, candid, sharp, amusing, full of his plans for writing and sketching and his comments on books and paintings. They include his famous long letter of 10 September 1864, in his second long vacation, on the three different kinds of poetic language: 'the language of inspiration', 'Parnassian' and 'Delphic'. The originality of Hopkins's views on poetry struck another contemporary, quoted by G.F. Lahey:

> His conversation was clever and incisive, and perhaps critical in excess. As to the quality of this criticism I thought much at the time, and have thought much since, that it was the best of the kind to be had in England, in places where production and criticism do not, as is the case at Oxford, keep pace. ... His acquaintance with poetry was extensive, and his judgements differed upon various poets considerably from what most people entertain.

Hopkins and Baillie remained very fond of each other, and on Hopkins's death Baillie wrote to Mrs Hopkins:

> It is impossible to say how much I owe to him. He is the one figure which fills my whole memory of my Oxford life. There is hardly a reminiscence with which he is not associated. All my intellectual growth, and a very large proportion of the happiness

of those Oxford days, I owe to his companionship. . . . Apart from my own nearest relatives, I never had so strong an affection for any one.

Other friends, close at the time, remain rather shadowy figures. Edward Bond, a scholar of St John's College, was Hopkins's companion on a holiday to Switzerland in 1868, and one of the few people to whom he showed his poems; but, like many of his Oxford friends, Bond dropped out of his life when Hopkins became a Jesuit.

Much the most important friendship Hopkins made at Oxford was with Robert Bridges. Although they did not meet until 1865, and only rarely after Hopkins had become a Jesuit, Hopkins's letters to Bridges make it clear of what crucial importance to him the friendship was. The letters, moreover—a substantial volume, edited in 1935 by Professor C.C. Abbott—tell us more about Hopkins's life and intellectual activity than any other source. For these reasons, the friendship with Bridges will be the subject of a separate section.

The letters to Baillie have plenty of the fun that endeared Luxmoore to Hopkins as a boy. It was to him that Hopkins sent the occasional vignette of a different side of Oxford life to what Geldart recorded of the Balliol scholars' table: 'We all got through Smalls [the qualifying examination]. Hardy . . . became light-headed, light-hearted, light-heeled. He, Brown and I proceeded to booze at the Mitre, and I forgot to pay my share, but I believe Hardy meant to feast us, in his delight.'

There are literary parodies, comic verses, and whimsical word-play in the two diaries Hopkins kept as an undergraduate too: 'Tuncks is a good name. Gerard Manley Tuncks. Pook Tuncks.' Besides normal jottings and memoranda, the diaries are filled with drafts and fragments of early poems; they show Hopkins's constant intellectual curiosity and the great range of his interests, particularly in art and architecture; and above all the excitement with words and the sensitivity to nature that characterized his whole life. The search for the essential form of a thing, and the exact words to express it, are here already: 'Grey clouds in knops. A curious fan of this kind of cloud radiating from a crown, and covering half the sky;' 'Whorled wave, whelked wave,—and drift;' 'Altogether *peak* is a good word. For sunlight through shutter, locks of hair, rays in brass knobs etc. Meadows peaked with flowers.' The numerous word lists and hazarded derivations of words are particularly interesting. They have an obvious connection with his classical studies; and one note at least shows that he had read Max Müller, the distinguished comparative philologist and Sanskrit scholar, then Professor of Modern European Languages in Oxford. But many of Hopkins's speculations were not only accurate, but original. 'What a philologist he might have made!' was the view of Alan Ward, who contributed the

Merton College, Oxford *by John Ruskin*

philological notes to *Hopkins's Journals and Papers*. Several of the key words in these diary entries appear in later poems; and often the associations he found between them clarify their later poetic use. The diaries are also filled with minute, delicately drawn architectural sketches, mostly illustrating notes on medieval or contemporary 'Gothic' churches. They clearly owe much to Ruskin and the medievalism of the High Church movement; but they also chart Hopkins's passion to communicate—if only to himself—to record in detail whatever he sees.

The tone of the last part of Hopkins's second diary, covering 1865, is very different. The poems and fragments are nearly all religious and in varying degrees sad or even anguished; he records his first known confession on Lady Day, 25 March, and thereafter keeps daily, often painfully scrupulous, confessional notes; the books he notes are mostly drawn from theological controversy. He was clearly undergoing a spiritual crisis, which led finally to his becoming a Roman Catholic the following year. Undoubtedly linked with the crisis, in a strong if not clear way, was his meeting with the seventeen-year-old poet Digby Mackworth Dolben that February. Hopkins's diary entries which follow closely on the meeting are significant: 'March 12. A day of the great mercy of God'; followed by his first recorded confession, 25 March; and, later that year: 'On this day by God's grace I resolved to give up all beauty until I had His leave for it; —also Dolben's letter came for which Glory to God.' An obscure but strongly felt sonnet written in his diary in April, 'Where art thou friend, whom I shall never see', was almost certainly addressed to Dolben.

Hopkins's first recorded confession in March 1865 was to Canon H.P. Liddon, who became his regular confessor; he also confessed that December to E.B. Pusey. These two strangely assorted men, both of Christ Church, were the acknowledged leaders of the High Church party in Oxford: Pusey much the older, one of the original Tractarians with Newman and Keble, a harsh, ascetic, but revered personality, embittered first by the loss of Newman to Rome, and then by the early death of his wife; and Liddon, his devoted friend and supporter, a much more serene and gentle personality, who exerted immense pastoral influence over undergraduates. Both men now heard private confessions regularly; although much earlier, in 1850, Pusey's hearing of them had led to his being inhibited from officiating as a priest in Oxford for two years. Bishop Wilberforce, who had inhibited him, had then described confession as 'the crowning curse' of Popery. Hopkins had come under Liddon's spell in his first term at Oxford, when he went to his Sunday evening lectures, followed by tea, coffee and talk. He was a member of Liddon's High Church essay society, the Hexameron. He was proposed and seconded for another High Church society, the Brother-hood of the Holy Trinity, of which Liddon was an active senior member and Pusey responsible for the rules; but, rather surprisingly, did not join it. Pusey's original rules, although not adopted, show the remarkable extent to which asceticism had permeated the High Church party, at any rate in Oxford: 'that the members should always walk with their eyes turned to the ground (as he did himself) or, failing that, wear round their loins a girdle of flannel as a token of self-restraint.'

One of the striking contradictions in Hopkins's character, mani-fested throughout his life and poetry, was between his asceticism and his keenly sensuous response to beauty. High Church Oxford certainly encouraged the former. His mother had already had to dissuade him from over-fasting; in November 1865 he had made his diary entry, resolving 'to give up all beauty' until he had God's leave for it; one of his last entries, early in 1866, was his programme for Lent:

> No pudding on Sundays. No tea except if to keep me awake and then without sugar. Meat only once a day. No verses in Passion Week or on Fridays. No lunch or meat on Fridays. Not to sit in armchair except can work in no other way. Ash Wednesday and Good Friday bread and water.

But, whatever emotions were involved in Hopkins's spiritual crisis, the stages by which he finally resolved to become a Roman Catholic were charted with intellectual precision. His diary entries, bunched together at the end of 1865, include references to F.G. Lee, a leading advocate for union between the Anglican and Roman Catholic Churches; and to two well-known converts to Rome: Provost Fortescue, who became a Catholic in 1871, and Frederick Oakley, a former Fellow of Balliol. But between the first two of these entries he copied out in full Newman's hymn, *Lead, kindly light*, written shortly before Newman's own conversion; and several of the poems and fragments of this second diary seem now almost a gloss on Newman's autobiographical novel, *Loss and Gain: the Story of a Convert*. Hopkins's own loss, like Newman's, was identified with Oxford; and one of two sonnets, *To Oxford*, that he wrote early in 1865 (and gave to William Addis), shows how sharp that loss must have been:

> New-dated from the terms that reappear,
> More sweet-familiar grows my love to thee,
> And still thou bind'st me to fresh fealty. . . .

> Those charms accepted of my inmost thought,
> The towers musical, quiet-walled grove . . .

This poignant love of Oxford is best remembered now in Matthew Arnold's famous description from his Preface to *Critical Essays*, 1865: 'whispering from her towers the last enchantments of the Middle Age. ... Home of lost causes and forsaken beliefs.' Arnold had also been a Balliol undergraduate; Hopkins was reading him in 1865 and heard him lecture as Professor of Poetry the following year. As Hopkins records long walks in and near Oxford with chosen friends in his 1866 Journal, we are strongly reminded of Arnold's *Thyrsis* and *The Scholar-Gipsy*. But Hopkins's thoughts were increasingly becoming anxieties about remaining an Anglican. In Lent he wrote a long poem, *Nondum* ('Not Yet'), reminiscent of Newman's *Lead, kindly light*; in May he recorded: 'Things look sad and difficult.' In June, during a walking tour in the West, he and Addis visited St Michael's, a Roman Catholic Benedictine monastery at Belmont, near Hereford. There they met Dom Paul Raynal, the first Catholic priest Hopkins ever spoke to, according to Addis. 'I think he made a great impression on both of us,' wrote Addis much later, 'and I believe that from that time our faith in Anglicanism was really gone.' Almost exactly four weeks later, Hopkins decided that he could not stay in the Church of England.

Conversion

Hopkins's Journal entry, recording his decision to become a Roman Catholic, was dated 17 July 1866. Its exactitude reflects his scrupulous personality: 'It was this night I believe but possibly the next that I saw clearly the impossibility of staying in the Church of England.' He was then spending a fortnight's holiday at a farm near Horsham, Sussex, with two Oxford friends, both High Church, William Garrett and William Comyn Macfarlane. The church services in the neighbourhood had played a large part in their choice of place; and although Hopkins described the farm as 'rather a fool's paradise, for the church is not what we expected and we are a long way off', when they were not reading or walking, they seem to have been in church. Although Hopkins had meant to keep his conversion secret for the time being, he incautiously told his two companions. 'Spoke to Macfarlane, foolishly', was his Journal entry for 24 July. Garrett became a Catholic himself shortly after hearing of Hopkins's conversion; Macfarlane kept his Anglican faith and was ordained that autumn.

During these two crucial weeks Hopkins was in an obvious state of tension ('we had a serious talk with Hopkins about his manners etc.', noted Macfarlane in his diary on 22 July); but his sense of wry fun was never long in abeyance. In a letter to Macfarlane, discussing the all-important question of nearby church services, Hopkins mocked his friend's excessive interest in High Church ritualism. In the same way he ended a serious letter to Bridges about his conversion, two months later, with characteristic self-mockery:

TRUMPERY,
MUMMERY, AND *G.M. HOPKINS* FLUMMERY
DESIGNER.
REMOVED TO THE OTHER SIDE OF THE WAY

Hopkins's conversion was only one out of several hundred in Oxford since Newman's conversion of twenty-one years before. It was one of five during the summer and autumn of 1866; and three of the other converts, William Addis, William Garrett and Alexander Wood, were Hopkins's close friends. As Hopkins wrote to Newman shortly before being received by him: 'All our minds you see were ready to go at a touch and it cannot but be that the same is the case with many here.' Enemies of the High Church party castigated this movement to Rome as the inevitable result of Tractarian teaching; for the Tractarians themselves, and particularly for Pusey, each new conversion was cause for fresh bitterness. As William Bright, one of Liddon's closest friends and supporters, wrote to Liddon, on hearing of the conversions of Hopkins and his friends: 'It is very deplorable. I cannot . . . believe that Hopkins, for instance, has made himself competent, in so grave & complex a question, to affirm the Roman position. . . . Meantime, of course, the Liberals . . . will be glad to welcome such a break-up in our junior ranks.'

But Hopkins was convinced that he *had* made himself competent. To Liddon, who wrote four letters in five days (16–20 October) pleading with him to delay, he stressed his logical reasoning and denied that he laid claim to any 'personal illumination': 'I can hardly believe anyone ever became a Catholic because two and two make four more fully than I have.' To his father who wrote (on 13 October) an agonized reply to his letter giving the news, he denied that 'fancy and aesthetic tastes had played any part': 'these wd. be better satisfied in the Church of England, for bad taste is always meeting one in the accessories of Catholicism.' What strikes us most forcibly throughout the crisis that followed his breaking the news to his parents, and to Pusey and Liddon, is his confidence, his clear conviction of the authority of the Church of Rome. Having accepted the arguments for that, there could be no going back. In long letters to his deeply distressed parents, he argued his position with relentless logic. Hardly surprisingly, his mother found him 'hard & cold'. His father, according to Hopkins, seemed to think that he was off his head and begged Liddon to 'save him from throwing a pure life and a somewhat unusual intellect away in the cold limbo which Rome assigns to her English converts'.

Hopkins's arguments about authority, that the Church of Rome was the only true Catholic Church, closely followed Newman's in his *Apologia*. It was to Newman, now at the Oratory in Birmingham, that he wrote late in August, asking for an interview and saying that his mind was made up. Newman saw him on 20 September and, as Hopkins wrote to Bridges, treated him with great kindness. And it was Newman who, after the week's crisis with his parents, received him into the Catholic Church at Birmingham on Sunday 21 October. Newman's kindness continued: unlike Archbishop Manning, he saw little sense in the official Catholic rule that undergraduate converts should not return to Oxford or Cambridge, and told Hopkins that his first duty was 'to make a good class'. He invited Hopkins to stay at the Oratory for Christmas, if there were difficulties about his going home; after his degree, in 1867, he offered him a teaching post at his Oratory School. For his part, Hopkins kept in touch with Newman for the rest of his life, and wrote to him every year on his birthday.

Although Hopkins stressed in all his letters the intellectual grounds for his conversion, it is clear that, inevitably, strong emotions were involved too, however rigorously kept under control. Such feelings are difficult to unravel. Dolben's involvement with Hopkins's first spiritual crisis has already been mentioned. A Journal entry made during Hopkins's walking-tour with William Addis (shortly to become a Catholic too), the day before Dom Paul Raynal made such an impression on them both, concerns friendship and associations of landscape with the past. Each of them was clearly undergoing a religious crisis; and it is difficult to believe that the conversation Hopkins recorded, and the feelings it summoned up, had not some connection with that crisis. 'Addis' idea of fondness or friendship he says is of feeling and not of acts of kindness', is the entry for 19 June. 'He thinks passing through a country associated with someone who has been before you ... is deeply sad, but it is not with associations of the dead./They are not dead who die, they are but lost who live.'

A visit Hopkins made only four days before his conversion may well have had personal and complicated motives, springing again from his sense of association. On 13 July, on his way to Horsham, he visited St Mary Magdalen's Church, West Lavington. He had earlier noted his interest in it as the work of Butterfield. But more important to him at this moment may have been the fact that the church was the gift of C.J. Laprimaudaye, Manning's former Anglican curate, confessor and intimate friend. Laprimaudaye became a Roman Catholic in 1850, before the church was finished, and was shortly followed by Manning himself. Laprimaudaye died in Rome in 1859, while studying for the priesthood.

Outwardly, Hopkins's life changed very little for some time after his reception. At Oxford he worked hard and successfully for 'Greats': one of his examiners, Professor Wilson, told Bridges: ' "For form" he was by far the best man in the first class.' His friendship with Bridges deepened. The rift with his parents to a great extent healed and he spent parts of his vacations with them. He travelled twice to the Continent: to Paris in July 1867 for a week; and to Switzerland the following July with Edward Bond for a month. In between, he taught at the Oratory School, Birmingham, as Newman had invited him to, for two terms; he liked the boys, but found the teaching increasingly burdensome. He seems to have written little if any poetry.

The first sign of his inner life comes in a long letter he wrote to Baillie from the school on 12 February 1868. After complaining of weak health, lack of time and energy, he writes:

> I am expecting to take orders and soon, but I wish it to be secret till it comes about. Besides that it is the happiest and best way it practically is the only one. You know I once wanted to be a painter. But even if I could I wd. not I think, now, for the fact is that the higher and more attractive parts of the art put a strain upon the passions which I shd. think it unsafe to encounter. I want to write still and as a priest I very likely can do that too, not so freely as I shd. have liked, e.g. nothing or little in the verse way, but no doubt what wd. best serve the cause of my religion. But if I am a priest it will cause my mother, or she says it will, great grief and this preys on my mind very much and makes the near prospect quite black.

The complaints about weak health and lack of energy recur many times in much later letters, when he was serving as a priest in Liverpool and Glasgow and teaching and examining in Dublin. There was much less obvious reason for them now. It is tempting to find their true cause in the struggle he must have undergone to abandon the writing of poetry; but the tone in which he refers to this to Baillie is one of, at worst, carefully articulated resignation. He must have known, too, that to become a priest would probably cause his mother less grief than his having become a Catholic. The real reason is surely one that he shared with George Herbert ('his strongest tie to the English Church', as William Addis wrote), who suffered acute illness on the brink of his ordination: in both cases an outward sign of the intense inner struggle that, in temperaments of Herbert's and Hopkins's fineness, preceded decisions of total dedication.

Before Hopkins left the Oratory School in April 1868, Father Henry Coleridge, S.J., a cousin of Hopkins's Highgate friend E.H. Coleridge, and a convert, gave the Holy Week retreat: he was almost certainly the first Jesuit priest Hopkins had met. What passed between them is not known; but Hopkins later referred to him as his oldest friend in the Society and from 27 April to 7 May Hopkins made a retreat with the Jesuits at Roehampton. During this retreat and the few days following, he made two decisions crucial to his future life. Before he returned home on 7 May, he had decided 'to be a priest and religious', but was still 'doubtful between St Benedict and St Ignatius'. By 12 May at the latest, he had chosen the Jesuits and had written to tell Newman. On 11 May he carried out a further, very personal, decision: to burn his poems. 'Slaughter of the innocents' is the enigmatic Journal entry, carefully cross-indexed with two earlier entries. As Humphry House convincingly showed, in an Appendix to *Journals and Papers*, this is its only possible interpretation. The cross-indexing shows that he had first made the resolution nearly nine months before, in the chapel of the Poor Clares, Notting Hill, but in a cautiously conditional form—'if it is better'. On 2 May the condition was dropped.

The burning itself was clearly a symbolic act, a sacrifice: much more important as evidence of his state of mind and of his intentions for the future, than in terms of what was destroyed. Both the letters in which he refers to the 'slaughter' make this clear. Telling Bridges that August that he had burnt his poems, he wrote: 'I saw they wd. interfere with my state and vocation.' And in the well-known letter to Canon Dixon of 5 October 1878 he told him: 'What I had written I burnt before I became a Jesuit and resolved to write no more, as not belonging to my profession, unless it were by the wish of my superiors.' Little that is unknown has probably perished: what has were mostly better drafts or finished versions of the poems in his two Oxford diaries, and the few poems (of which he had already sent MSS to Bridges) written after January 1866. But, apart from 'two or three little presentation pieces which occasion called for', his self-imposed silence was kept: he wrote no more poetry until 'The Wreck of the *Deutschland*' in December 1875.

Hopkins's decision to join the Jesuits and their acceptance of him on 30 May brought him, as he told his friend William Urquhart, 'the first complete peace of mind I have ever had'. A few days earlier he had written to Liddon: 'I am going to enter the Jesuit noviciate at Roehampton: I do not think there is another prospect so bright in the world.' The writing of poetry he had for the time abandoned; but the month that he now spent on the Continent with Edward Bond, mainly in Switzerland, before going to Roehampton on 7 September, produced its own evidence of his new frame of mind: some of his fullest, most vivid and happiest Journal-writing.

2 Religious background

Oxford religious controversies of the 1860s

In June 1864, after his first year at Balliol, Hopkins wrote to his school-friend E.H. Coleridge, hoping that he would come up to Oxford soon and become more 'Catholic': a state easier to achieve 'when you are come to the head and fount of Catholicism in England and the heart of our Church'. 'Our Church' was, of course, the Anglo-Catholic Church, the Church of the Tractarians, so called from the *Tracts for the Times* published in Oxford between 1833 and 1841 by the leaders of the party for spiritual reform within the Anglican Church—in particular by J.H. Newman, John Keble, and Newman's disciple, W.G. Ward (of Balliol). How closely Hopkins identified himself with it—and with its new Oxford leaders, E.B. Pusey and H.P. Liddon—is clear from the letter he wrote to his father in October 1866, justifying his conversion to Rome: 'The Tractarian ground I have seen broken to pieces under my feet. . . . Dr Pusey and Mr Liddon were the only two men in the world who cd. avail to detain me . . . when that influence gave way everything was gone.' This disillusion with the Tractarians is the background to his increasingly strained religious poetry at Oxford and to his conversion.

Hopkins's sad (or defiant) comment to his father was justified: by 1866 most of the Tractarian ground had indeed been lost. The enemy now, seemingly ever more triumphant, was infidelity, the 'wilder beast from West' of Hopkins's later sonnet, *Andromeda*. But the first and clearest enemy had been Rome. Keble's giving up of his Fellowship of Oriel College in 1823 and his final departure from Oxford in 1836 to become a country Rector, had been sad blows to the original Oxford Movement. Newman's conversion to Rome in 1845 was an infinitely worse one. The stream of conversions since was a constant distress to the Movement's successors. But the Tractarians' spirit was preserved, indeed intensified, by Keble's intimate friend and supporter of his ideals, E.B. Pusey. Pusey had joined the Tractarians in 1834; after Keble's departure, he was the acknowledged leader, joined in 1859 by H.P. Liddon. These two men, with their followers, set themselves to preserve the true Christian faith against infidelity. Signs of infidelity they found everywhere in English society, but in Oxford, with its profound influence over the hearts and minds of Britain's most susceptible youth, they found it at its most threatening in the new scientific spirit. Such a spirit was dangerous everywhere; it came to be so most dramatically, of course, in the scientists themselves. Darwin's *Origin of Species* was published in 1859; T.H. Huxley's routing of Samuel Wilberforce, the Bishop of Oxford, took place in Oxford itself a year later. But this new spirit was doubly dangerous when it was combined with the dedication, even piety, of men like Thomas Arnold of Rugby, Jowett of Balliol, and eminent Churchmen like Arthur Stanley, Dean of Westminster, and Charles Kingsley, Professor of Modern History at Cambridge since 1860 (whose proposed honorary degree the Oxford High Church party succeeded in thwarting). These were the leaders of the so-called Broad Church party, and they epitomized everything the Tractarians most disliked and feared: above all, personal interpretation of the Bible; 'neology', adherence to the new German scriptural scholarship; and speculation in ideas.

At Oxford the struggle became almost a personal one between Pusey and Jowett; and during the 1850s Jowett undoubtedly had the worst of it. In 1854 he lost the election to the Mastership of Balliol largely because of his unorthodox religious views. In December 1855 he was denounced, not by Pusey, but by two Evangelicals, for his 'Essay on the Atonement' in his *Commentary on the Pauline Epistles*; summoned by the Vice-Chancellor, he submitted by signing the 'Articles of Religion'. 'Hereticus', as Jowett now referred to himself to his friend Dean Stanley, was virtually silent—on these issues at least—for the next four years.

But in 1860 'the march of mind' (to the Tractarians, the march of infidelity) moved inexorably on. In February was published *Essays and Reviews*, a symposium of scholarly, searching essays by seven Broad Churchmen ('Septem contra Christum', as the Tractarians branded them). Jowett's own contribution, 'On the Interpretation of Scripture', was a closely argued plea of 100 pages for the use of reason. All were influenced by German scholarship and the new scientific spirit. To the Tractarians they were the final undermining of the sacred citadel of Faith, the Bible. They led to the greatest religious controversy of the century; and to the ultimate defeat, both in the courts and in the forum of public opinion, of the Tractarians.

Pusey and his followers tried every means in their power to have *Essays and Reviews* and its authors condemned as heretical. In the highest ecclesiastical court, the Court of Arches, and in Convocation, they were successful: two contributors were suspended as priests for a year and the book was synodically condemned. But in February 1863 (two months before Hopkins came up to Balliol), an attempt by Pusey to have Jowett charged with heresy before the Vice-Chancellor failed; and a year later the Privy Council upheld the appeals of the two convicted contributors. One of the charges against them was that they had denied the doctrine of eternal damnation: as a mock epitaph on Lord Westbury, President of the Court, put it, he had, in refusing to uphold the conviction, 'dismissed Hell with costs'.

Meanwhile the Church—and the country—were shaken even more by the extraordinary case of Bishop Colenso of Natal. Colenso, worried by the questions of some of his Zulu flock, had himself asked fundamental questions in two books on the Epistle to the Romans and the Pentateuch. His 'Metropolitan', the High Church Bishop Gray of Cape Town, then (quite illegally) himself condemned him for heresy. In March 1865 the Privy Council upheld Colenso's appeal. Nothing daunted, Gray excommunicated him and appointed a rival Bishop; Colenso, regarding himself (lawfully) as the true Bishop, remained in his see till his death in 1883.

In Oxford itself Jowett had the majority support of the Fellows of Balliol by 1865. That February Christ Church, submitting finally to intense pressure, raised his scandalously low salary as Professor of Greek from £40 to £500 p.a. In 1870 his election as Master of Balliol set the seal on the victory of the spirit and the path he stood for.

Surprisingly, Hopkins has only two explicit references to this momentous struggle within the Church: a memorandum in his Diary to read *Essays and Reviews*, and a question in a letter as to what was happening in the Colenso case. But without a doubt he was keenly aware of the implications of both. When he made his decision to leave the Church of England, the Tractarian ground—at any rate as a base of power within the Church—had indeed been 'broken to pieces'; and the influence of Pusey and Liddon must have seemed sadly on the wane.

The 'Spiritual Exercises'

From 7 September 1868, the day that Hopkins joined the Jesuit Novitiate, to the day of his death, the *Spiritual Exercises* of St Ignatius were the centre of his spiritual life. Composed by Ignatius Loyola, the Spanish founder of the Society of Jesus, in Manresa between 1521 and 1541, they had and have not changed. In four weeks' meditations they help the Jesuit to dedicate his life to Christ, as Ignatius himself had done; to order his life, as a whole and daily, according to God's will for him. During his whole life as a Jesuit, Hopkins studied the *Exercises*, meditated on them, and lived them. His most important spiritual writing was part of a Commentary on them; his most intimate writing, 'Notes on Retreats', was given up to their practice. The *Spiritual Exercises* had a profound effect on his life, thought and feeling, and on his poetry.

Hopkins's notes towards a Commentary on the *Exercises*, made mostly during his Long Retreat in Winter 1881, show how close his spirit had become to that of St Ignatius. Ignatius's own ideal, as befitted his past life as a soldier, was that of service to Christ seen as the love and dedication of a medieval knight to his Sovereign; through grace, the obedient and self-sacrificing servant can become *alter Christus*, another Christ. Two of his meditations, on the Kingdom of Christ and on the Two Standards (the standard of Christ and the standard of Satan—there is no compromise), are full of military images. Gentle by temperament, Hopkins, through his will and imagination, seized on this central Ignatian image of the Jesuit as Christ's totally dedicated soldier. Christ's great sacrifice (the subject of the final two weeks' meditations) permeates his Commentary, his sermons and some of his letters. Christ's beauty is the subject of his finest sermon. The story of Christ's Passion affected him profoundly.

The *Spiritual Exercises* open with Ignatius's statement of creation, the Principle or Foundation: 'Man was created to praise, reverence and serve God Our Lord, and by so doing to save his soul.' This belief governed Hopkins's life. His Commentary begins with a long examination of its first three words, *Homo creatus est*. Creation passes naturally, for Hopkins, from the world without to 'ourselves the world within'; and there follows one of the finest, most individually distinctive, of his spiritual writings, on 'self being'. Its philosophical purpose is to prove that such distinctive being can only have been created by 'one of finer or higher pitch and determination than itself', by God. But contemplation of the miracle of selfhood brings Hopkins's imaginative energy into full play.

> I find myself both as man and as myself something most determined and distinctive, at pitch, more distinctive and higher pitched than anything else I see; I find myself with my pleasures and pains, my powers and my experiences, my deserts and guilt, my shame and sense of beauty, my dangers, hopes, fears, and all my fate, more important to myself than anything I see. And when I ask where does all this throng and stack of being, so rich, so distinctive, so important, come from/nothing I see can answer me. And this whether I speak of human nature or of my individuality, my selfbeing. ... And this is much more true when we consider the mind; when I consider my selfbeing; my consciousness and feeling of myself, that taste of myself, of *I* and *me* above and in all things, which is more distinctive than the taste of ale or alum, more distinctive than the smell of walnutleaf or camphor, and is incommunicable by any means to another man (as when I was a child I used to ask myself: What must it be to be someone else?) Nothing else in nature comes near this unspeakable stress of pitch, distinctiveness, and selving, this selfbeing of my own. ... searching nature I taste *self* but at one tankard, that of my own being. The development, refinement, condensation of nothing shews any sign of being able to match this to me or give me another taste of it, a taste even resembling it.

Three years later, in Dublin, when Hopkins was at his lowest ebb, he returned to Ignatius's Foundation Exercise in one of his points for meditation. Humphry House, the first editor of Hopkins's *Notebooks and Papers*, describes the entry in what is now known as 'the Dublin Notebook':

> In the last sentences [*beginning 'Man was created'*] he stopped on the word 'created' and wrote it again, twice the size, in a huge, sprawling, childlike hand; crossed it out, began again 'cr' still bigger, crossed that out too, and in the same hand wrote 'crea'. ... The next page is completely filled with √s, made as he marked [examination] papers.

It is as if in the weariness of examining and the nervous exhaustion Hopkins suffered in Dublin, he had somehow to proclaim again to himself Ignatius's principle of creation.

The rest of the Foundation Exercise lays down 'the proper use of creatures': they 'were created for man's sake and to help him in the carrying out of the end for which he was created. ... man should make use of creatures so far as they help him to attain his end'. In his Further Notes Hopkins comments: 'This world then is word, expression, views of God. ... the world, man, should after its own manner give God being in return for the being he has given it'. All creatures lead back to their creator, God. This is the sacramental view of nature and it is central to Hopkins's poetry.

If the spirit of much of Hopkins's poetry is Ignatian, its structure seems equally so. The essence of the Ignatian meditation is 'to see with the eyes of the imagination'. It has three basic elements. First, the exercitant (or meditator) must 'compose the place', re-create the subject of the meditation—be it the joys of Christ's Kingdom or the Crucifixion or his own sins—in his own imagination, in vivid detail; next, he must use fully 'the three powers': memory, to recall the subject; understanding, to reflect on and analyse it; and will, to turn reflection into virtuous action; finally, he must enter into a 'colloquy' with God or Christ on the chosen subject (as Hopkins put it in his Commentary: 'The Colloquy is made properly by speaking as a friend to a friend, or as a servant to his master'). Throughout, he must make the fullest use of all his senses to *realize* the subject dramatically, to bring it home—with its joys or sorrows or terrors —to his imagination. The nearness of this to some kinds of poetry is clear; and in *The Poetry of Meditation*, Louis Martz has shown convincingly how the Ignatian meditation lies behind much seventeenth-century religious poetry.

George Herbert (for whom Hopkins had a particular affection) and John Donne, in his *Holy Sonnets*, undoubtedly drew on the Ignatian meditation; so equally did Hopkins. It is one of the sources of power, both sensuous and dramatic, of almost all the poems he wrote as a Jesuit. The inspiration of the opening section of *The Deutschland* was his first experience of the *Spiritual Exercises*, the meditations that governed his Long Retreat as a novice seven years before. The exultant 1877 sonnets, written in Wales, follow closely the pattern of the Ignatian meditation: having celebrated the wonder of starlight night or harvest or windhover, they turn the beauty they reflect on into virtuous action or affection; meditation has led, as it should, to spiritual act or energy. The agony of the most desolate of the Dublin sonnets is that this does not happen; the final phase has failed. They begin as meditations on Hopkins's own suffering and helplessness; they end, not in action, but paralysis.

Hopkins was greatly concerned with the structure of the sonnet itself: he continually comments on the form of his sonnets to both Bridges and Dixon. As Martz has pointed out, the traditional Petrarchan sonnet—the basic form Hopkins used most—in its 4-4-6 line division, in fact mirrors the threefold structure of the Ignatian meditation. But ultimately the form or shape of a poem had a more intimate, and perhaps more important, justification to Hopkins. He felt intensely that it was made in that form to praise Christ: a new creation, another of His works, with a pattern distinctively its own. In writing it, the poet has in his own way carried out the first and vital exercise of the *Spiritual Exercises*: 'Man was created to praise.'

Duns Scotus

There are three references in Hopkins's *Journals* to the thirteenth-century Franciscan philosopher Duns Scotus (1266–1308), nick-named 'the Subtle Doctor', to whom he referred in a sermon on the Immaculate Conception as 'the greatest of the divines and doctors of the Church who have spoken and written in favour of the truth'; and he wrote a moving sonnet, *Duns Scotus's Oxford* (where Scotus had both studied and lectured), to show his especial devotion to him. To Bridges, who recommended that he should read Hegel, he wrote in 1875: 'After all I can, at all events a little, read Duns Scotus and I care for him more even than Aristotle and more *pace tua* than a dozen Hegels.' There is no doubt that Scotus had a profound influence on Hopkins's thought; above all, that he corroborated, within a Catholic framework, some of Hopkins's own most distinctive ideas.

Scotus's main distinction from the traditional theology taught to Jesuits (that of Francisco Suarez, based on St Thomas Aquinas) was his belief in the 'principle of individuation', both of persons and things. All medieval philosophers were concerned with how human beings could come to know the universal; Scotus believed that they could do so by apprehending an individual object's essence, which he named its 'this-ness' (*haecceitas*); and that such apprehensions or intuitions ultimately reveal God. By directing such intuitions of nature towards God man can perfect his own *haecceitas*, his will. Here seemed to be philosophical support for Hopkins's theories of inscape and instress, and a religious sanction for them.

It was at Stonyhurst in August 1872 that Hopkins first read Scotus.

> At this time [he recorded], I had first begun to get hold of the copy of Scotus on the Sentences in the Baddely library and was flush with a new stroke of enthusiasm. It may come to nothing or it may be a mercy from God. But just then when I took in any inscape of the sky or sea I thought of Scotus.

A year later he 'talked Scotism ... for the last time' with a fellow-Jesuit; and in July 1874 he met two further Scotists, 'so that oddly I made the acquaintance of two and I suppose the only two Scotists in England in one week'.

Scotus's belief in the principle of individuation clearly lies behind Hopkins's commentary on the opening of the *Spiritual Exercises*, already quoted, with its great celebration of selfhood. Two sonnets in particular show the strength that Hopkins's poetry gained from him: *Henry Purcell* and *As kingfishers catch fire*. Both explore and celebrate self-distinctiveness. Purcell's music utters, as Hopkins's epitaph to the sonnet puts it, 'the very make and species of man as created both in him and in all men generally'. *As kingfishers catch fire* goes further. 'The very make and species of man', for Hopkins— as for Scotus—was ultimately Christ Incarnate; so the poem ends with man's truest 'selving', his becoming—through grace—*alter Christus*, Christ Himself:

> Acts in God's eye what in God's eye he is—
> Christ—for Christ plays in ten thousand places,
> Lovely in limbs, and lovely in eyes not his
> To the Father through the features of men's faces.

One of Scotus's theological teachings was that Christ's incarnation was not dependent on the Fall, on man's sin, but a free choice, an act of love: 'I say then that the Fall was not the reason for Christ's predestination. Even if no angel had fallen, nor any man, Christ would still have been predestined.' Christ's 'great sacrifice', then, was an act of love, freely chosen; and it is this love that man, at his highest, should imitate. This again profoundly influenced Hopkins's thought. Hopkins's strong love of the Virgin Mary almost certainly also owed something to Duns Scotus: in a sermon of 1879 he referred glowingly to Scotus's traditional public defence of the Immaculate Conception in Paris. His sonnet, *Duns Scotus's Oxford*, written the same year, shows his love of, and deep sense of kinship with, both the philosopher and the theologian.

There is a tradition that Hopkins's Scotism 'got him into difficulties with his Jesuit preceptors', and that this played a part in what Christopher Devlin has called the first of the 'three wounds' to his 'expectation of a full and useful life' as a priest: his not being, as he had expected, promoted to a further year of theological studies after his ordination. The tradition is not documented; but, true or not, it seems of less importance than the sense of fulfilled need given by the hero of *Duns Scotus's Oxford:* he

> who of all men most sways my spirits to peace;
> Of realty the rarest-veined unraveller; a not
> Rivalled insight, be rival Italy or Greece;
> Who fired France for Mary without spot.

Hopkins and the Society of Jesus

'Don't call "the Jesuit discipline hard", it will bring you to heaven. The Benedictines would not have suited you.' Thus Newman did his best to allay Hopkins's apprehensions about becoming a Jesuit, on his decision to do so in May 1868. Many people since have felt that Hopkins's fears were justified: that the rigorous discipline of the Jesuits was ill-suited to his peculiarly sensitive gifts; that the vocation of the Jesuit priest was bound to destroy the vocation of the poet. The evidence of Hopkins's letters points firmly to his never regretting, even in his darkest, most frustrated days, his decision to enter the Society of Jesus. Three years after the decision, he used an unforgettable phrase to Baillie to describe his new life: 'This life here [at Stonyhurst] though it is hard is God's will for me as I most intimately know, which is more than violets knee-deep.' When he was preparing to take his final vows he was absolutely firm, if self-deprecating: 'I have never wavered in my vocation, but I have not lived up to it.'

Of the Jesuit vocation itself he was intensely proud. 'My vocation puts before me a standard so high that a higher can be found nowhere else', he wrote to Dixon. He was proud of the Jesuits' sanctity; of their persecution (he began an ode on the martyrdom of Edmund Campion, but—sadly—laid it aside); of their dedication to God's will. Bridges's dislike of the Catholics, and of the Jesuits in particular, hurt him greatly. He could be sharply sarcastic in defence: 'You say you don't like Jesuits. Did you ever see one?' He could joke about the Society's reputation: 'The Puseyites are up to some very dirty jesuitical tricks.' But he could also show how Bridges had wounded him. 'It is long since such things had any significance for you', he wrote, after Bridges had clearly written disparagingly of the Corpus Christi procession at Roehampton. 'But what is strange and unpleasant is that you sometimes speak as if they had in reality none for me and you were only waiting with a certain disgust till I too should be disgusted with myself enough to throw off the mask.'

Hopkins was a Jesuit for almost half his life; his mature poems were written either shortly before he was ordained a priest or during his varied ministries. A brief sketch of the Jesuits in England, followed by a short account of his nine-year training for the priesthood, seems therefore essential to complete his background.

The Jesuits in England

The history of the Jesuits in England, for almost the three centuries up to the year of Hopkins's ordination, 1877, is one of persecution. The first small party of about a dozen, including the poet Edmund Campion, arrived from Rome in 1580, intent on the reconversion of England, even if it could only be achieved by the overthrow of Elizabeth and the help of Spain. They arrived in disguise and with aliases; were hunted down as traitors; and on 1 December 1581 Campion himself, with two of the others, was hanged at Tyburn. 'The very day 300 years ago of Father Campion's martyrdom', Hopkins headed a letter to Dixon on 1 December 1881; and he expected from it some 'great conversion or other blessing to the Church in England'. The Jesuit 'mission' to England remained; indeed, despite—or because of—persecution, it expanded rapidly. There were eight further executions under Elizabeth (including that of another poet, Robert Southwell, in 1595); four more (including that of Henry Garnet, Superior of the mission) in 1606 after the Gunpowder Plot; but within a further twenty years the number of English Jesuits had increased to 300.

Persecution undoubtedly played a part in attracting some of the more idealistic recruits. Hopkins himself commented on the expulsion of the Spanish Jesuits in 1868: 'To be persecuted in a tolerant age is a high distinction.' This was something that St Ignatius had foreseen. As summarized by one of Hopkins's contemporary Jesuits, R.F. Clarke, Ignatius

> used to beg of God that his followers might always be the object of the world's hatred and enmity. He told them that they should wish to suffer contumely, false accusations and insults,—so long as they themselves gave no sort of occasion for it, and no offence is thereby committed against the Divine Majesty.

He regarded 'persecution and misrepresentation as a necessary accompaniment of every victory won for the sacred cause of Christianity'.

For the rest of the seventeenth century the English Jesuits lived in hiding: enforced obscurity, to some extent, saved them from further persecution. Behind the scenes, they organized the first English Province of the Society, most of their recruits now being trained at English Jesuit Colleges in Flanders: at St Omers, Louvain, Liège, Watten, Ghent. But active persecution was never far away: it returned in full force with the so-called Popish Plot of 1680. Eight years later the Jesuits were in the van of James II's Catholic supporters imprisoned or exiled at the Glorious Revolution.

The pattern of these penal days was much the same for most of the next century. Jesuits remained in England, but again in hiding, many serving as chaplains to Catholic families. There could be no open Jesuit communities; but individual priests, even in hiding, were still members of the Society and still practised the Jesuit life. That came to an end in 1773. In August of that year Pope Clement XIV gave way to twenty years' pressure by Pombal, dictator of Portugal, supported by much other hostility to the Jesuits throughout Europe, and published a Papal Brief suppressing the Society. The English Jesuits were, of course, suppressed with the rest; most of them remained in England and served as diocesan priests. Twenty-one years later, in June 1794, the French Revolution drove the former Jesuit staff and their pupils from the college at Liège; by that October they were settled in Stonyhurst, Lancashire, given to them by Thomas Weld.

The history of the eventual restoration of the Society in England is a complex one. By political chance, the White Russian Jesuits had alone escaped the suppression, as subjects, since the Partition of Poland, of Catherine the Great of Russia. The English ex-Jesuits were able to affiliate with them, and in 1803 were given verbal permission by the Pope to re-form the Society in private. In August 1814 Pope Pius VII restored the Jesuits publicly. But the English Jesuits had to wait for another thirteen years. They had powerful enemies among English Catholics as well as a hostile English Government; and it was not until 1827 that Pope Leo XII formally ruled their restoration.

By the mid-nineteenth century the Society was already much as Hopkins knew it. Despite a penal clause in the Catholic Emancipation Act of 1829, forbidding the recruitment of Jesuits, numbers increased rapidly. There were 112 English Jesuits in 1833; 347 in 1870, when Hopkins was a novice; and nearly 600 in 1890, the year after his death. The only effect of the clause was that in the 1860s novices, including Hopkins, pronounced their first vows in secrecy. In 1833 Jesuit education was virtually confined to Stonyhurst. In 1854 the novices moved first to Beaumont Lodge, near Windsor, then to Roehampton in 1861. St Beuno's College, near St Asaph, in North Wales, where Hopkins did his theology, was founded in 1848. The Jesuits were now especially active in facing the effects of the Industrial Revolution, particularly in the new industrial towns in the North, swamped by waves of poor Catholic Irish immigrants. They created new missions and new schools for the sons of the Catholic poor; and these, with the often appalling problems they brought with them, included the parishes and the school in which Hopkins served: Mount

St Mary's College, Chesterfield; St Joseph's, Bedford Leigh, near Manchester; St Francis Xavier's, Liverpool; St Joseph's, Glasgow.

A final point should be made about the rapid Victorian expansion of the Jesuits. For the first time, they included many converts: disciples of Newman and Manning and some, like Hopkins himself, of Pusey and Liddon. Several of Hopkins's fellow-novices were typical of many who had given up promising careers to join the Society: Henry Schomberg Kerr, Commander, RN; John Walford, who had taught at Eton for five years; Richard Clarke, Fellow and Tutor of St John's College, Oxford, with whom Hopkins was at St Beuno's. A Society that had survived three centuries of persecution and obscurity, and remained intact, had remarkable resilience; such recruits as these brought a particular kind of maturity and dedication to the Victorian Jesuits.

The novitiate: Roehampton, 1868–70

Manresa House, Roehampton, had been the Jesuit novitiate for seven years only when Hopkins arrived to spend his two years as a novice there, from 7 September 1868 to 8 September 1870. The training was virtually the same as it had been in Rome or Flanders, during the penal days: each stage a rigorous test of the novice's vocation for the Jesuit life. The new novices begin with a probationary period of about a week, separated from the rest. R.F. Clarke, a novice three years after Hopkins, described the purpose of this period in 'The training of a Jesuit' (*The Nineteenth Century*, August 1869):

> The rules of the Society are put into their hands, and are explained to them; they are instructed as to the kind of life they will have to live, and the difficulties that they will have to encounter. They have to study the 'Summary of the Constitutions', in which is set forth the end and object of the Society, the spirit that must animate its members, the obedience they must be ready to practise, the sacrifice of their own will and judgment that they must be prepared to make; in fact, they have every possible opportunity given them of ascertaining what it is that they are undertaking when they declare their intention of serving God in the Society according to its laws and constitutions.

After a short retreat, they are accepted as novices and receive the Jesuit habit.

The next and most exacting test of vocation was the Long Retreat, begun by Hopkins and his fellow-novices on 16 September, a month earlier than it would be today. This was their first introduction to St Ignatius's *Spiritual Exercises*. Clarke thus describes it:

Manresa House, Roehampton

It consists of thirty days occupied exclusively in prayer, meditation, and similar employments. Five times a day the master of novices gives points of meditation to the assembled novices, and they have subsequently to spend the following hour in a careful pondering over the points proposed to them. .... A regular system is followed; during the first few days the subjects proposed are the end for which man is created, the means by which he is to attain that end, the evils of sin and its consequences, and the four last things, death, judgment, heaven, and hell. During the second portion of the retreat the Kingdom of Christ, His Incarnation, Nativity, and His life on earth occupy the thoughts of the novices for a space of ten or twelve days, with separate meditations on the two standards of Christ and Satan, under one of which every one is fighting, on the tactics of the evil one, the choice that has to be bravely made of a life of hardship under the standard of the Cross, and other subjects akin to these. During a third period of four or five days the Passion of Christ is dwelt upon in detail, and finally some two or three days of the joyful subjects of the Resurrection, the appearances of our Lord to his disciples, the Ascension, with one or two concluding meditations on the love of God and the means of attaining it, bring the retreat to an end.

Except for three recreation days, spent in long walks, silence is kept throughout.

The novice's vocation was also tested more practically by what were called 'experiments': the taking of catechism classes, attending the sick in hospitals, going on pilgrimages or missionary journeys. They emphasize that the Jesuit aim is both personal sanctity and service to God through deeds. They also train the novice in obedience, the characteristic Jesuit virtue. In Hopkins's time such 'experiments' were limited to catechizing children in neighbouring parishes: Isleworth, Brentford, Fulham, Marylebone. For his last three months as a novice he was in charge of the classes in Marylebone. The novices also preached their first sermons, or 'tones', as they are called, within the community itself. Hopkins preached on the Feast of St Stanislaus (13 November) 1869; and his sermon was later remembered as 'brilliant and beautiful'.

The novices live in small, austerely furnished cubicles; and we know from Clarke the timetable that Hopkins and his six fellow-novices followed. They rose at 5.30, briefly visited the chapel at 6.00, meditated from 6.00 to 7.00, celebrated Mass at 7.00, and from 7.30 to 7.45 reconsidered their meditation. After breakfast at 7.45, they read, individually, *Rodriguez on Christian Perfection*, from 8.30 to 9.00. At 9.00 they were instructed on the rules of the Society by the novice-master, then made their beds, tidied their cubicles, and carried out domestic tasks. At 10.15 they learnt by heart a portion of the Society's rules or prayers or psalms. At 10.30 they were given free time to walk in the grounds, pray in the chapel, or read a spiritual book; and from 11.30 to 12.30 they did outdoor manual work (sawing wood, sweeping leaves, etc.). They then spent fifteen minutes in chapel, praying, and examining their consciences concerning their performance of the morning's duties. Dinner was at 1.0, during which portions of the Bible and of a spiritual book were read aloud. After a short visit to the chapel, they were given an hour's recreation, followed by either outdoor manual work or a two-hour walk with one or two other novices chosen by the novice-master. Sometimes they played cricket or football instead. At 6.00 they meditated again in chapel and recited prayers. After some free time, supper was at 7.30. At 8.00 there was an hour's recreation, during the first half-hour of which Latin had to be spoken; at 9.00 prayers in chapel, followed by preparation of their meditation for the next morning and a final examination of conscience. Lights out at 10.00.

Despite this rigorous routine, many of the novices wished to do extra penances; but for these the novice-master's permission had to be obtained. Hopkins was not allowed to fast in Lent 1869; but he was given permission for a custody-of-the-eyes penance (i.e. looking downwards for most of the time) from January to July of that year. It 'prevented', his Journal starkly records, 'my seeing much that half-year'.

In December 1869 Hopkins was made 'Porter', or chief novice, for ten weeks. One of his duties was to record in a journal the routine events of each day. The journal is given complete by Fr Alfred Thomas in *Hopkins the Jesuit*. The very baldness of the entries conveys strikingly, as Fr Thomas says, what life in the noviceship was like. The monotony itself was part of the training in obedience. But such a routine account disguises the intense mental and spiritual activity brought into play by the daily meditation, examination of conscience, and spiritual reading. Some novices decided during the novitiate that they had insufficient vocation to continue. Hopkins never wavered. But a Journal entry at the beginning of 1870 gives us a glimpse of his spiritual state. During the Long Retreat they had been reading in the refectory the account of the Agony in the Garden written by Sister Anne Catherine Emmerich (1774–1824), the German visionary, in her book *The Dolorous Passion of Our Lord Jesus Christ*. Hopkins records: 'I suddenly began to cry and sob and could not stop . . . I remember much the same thing on Maundy Thursday when the presanctified Host was carried to the sacristy.'

On 8 September the novices took their vows of perpetual poverty, chastity and obedience, in secret, in a tiny chapel, kneeling in front of the novice-master. Hopkins left for Stonyhurst the next morning. Writing to his mother the following day, feeling the strangeness of the new place, he told her that 'the noviceship after two years seems like a second home'.

The seminary: St Mary's Hall, Stonyhurst, 1870–73

St Mary's Hall, the Jesuit seminary for the three-year training in philosophy, was established in 1835. Though a close dependency of Stonyhurst College nearby, it was a separate community of thirty-five scholastics under its own Superior. Hopkins was there from 9 September 1870 to 29 August 1873. Much of the religious routine was as at Roehampton. Instead of cubicles, the scholastics had their own sparsely-furnished rooms. They rose at 5.30, meditated and attended Mass until breakfast; had a short examination of conscience before dinner at 1.00; and further prayers and examination of conscience until bed at 10.15. Study occupied most of the day. They had lectures (in Latin) from 10.00 to 12.30; studies from 5.00 to 8.00; and, on three days a week, from 3.15 to 4.15, an academical exercise known as 'the circle'.

During their first year they studied logic, mathematics, and probably some metaphysics; in their second and third years, psychology, ethics, metaphysics, cosmology and natural theology. The philosophy taught in Hopkins's time was narrowly neo-Thomist: almost certainly St Thomas as interpreted by the Jesuit theologian Franciso Suarez. The Professors teaching these courses in Hopkins's day were

St Mary's Hall, Stonyhurst

German and Italian: few English Jesuits were yet equipped to do so. The scholastics were examined orally each year, the third year *de universa philosophia* in Latin.

'The circle' is thus described by R.F. Clarke in his 'Training of a Jesuit':

> Besides the lectures, which are given in Latin, the students are summoned three times a week to take part in an academical exercise which is one of the most valuable elements in the philosophical and theological training of the Society. It lasts an hour, during the first quarter of which one of the students has to give a synopsis of the last two lectures of the professor. After this, two other students, previously appointed for the purpose, have to bring against the doctrine laid down any possible objection that they can find in books or invent for themselves. . . . Everything has to be brought forward in syllogistic form, and to be answered in the same way. The professor, who of course presides at these contests, at once checks any one who departs from this necessary form and wanders off into mere desultory talk. This system of testing the soundness of the doctrine taught, continued as it is throughout the theological studies which come at a later period of the young Jesuit's career, provides those who pass through it with a complete defence against difficulties which otherwise are likely to puzzle the Catholic controversialist. . . .
>
> When the two objicients have finished their attack, there still

remains a quarter of an hour before the circle is over. This time is devoted to objections and difficulties proposed by the students. Every one present has full freedom to ask of the professor any question he pleases on the matter in hand, and may require of him an explanation of any point on which he is not satisfied. It is needless to say that full advantage is taken of this privilege, and the poor professor has often to submit to a very lively and searching interrogatory. If any question is proposed that is foolish, or beside the subject, the questioner is soon silenced by the open marks of disapprobation on the part of rest of the class, and a good objection is sometimes received with quiet applause. Any fallacy or imperfect knowledge on the part of the professor is very speedily brought to light by the raking fire he has to undergo, and while all respect is shown him in the process, he must be well armed if he is to win the confidence of the class by his answers.

The philosophy course was clearly an exacting one, as even Hopkins, with his Oxford Greats training behind him, found. He told Baillie in April 1871 that he was 'going through a hard course of scholastic logic ... which takes all the fair part of the day and leaves one fagged at the end for what remains. This makes the life painful to nature'; and in December of the next year: 'I am here for another year and now they are having at me with ethics and mechanics ... I spent a miserable morning over formulas for the lever.' No doubt because of this, more, and more varied, recreation was allowed than at Roehampton. There was bathing throughout the summer 'at a beautiful spot in the Hodder all between waterfalls and beneath a green meadow', as Hopkins described it to his mother; cricket against the Stonyhurst lay-philosophers; salmon fishing; and at Christmas, skating on the Stonyhurst pond by torchlight and Chinese lanterns, and plays and music in the refectory (one such entertainment being arranged by Hopkins). There were also annual two-week holidays, or 'Villas', in Argyllshire and the Isle of Man and monthly free days, or 'Blandykes' (named after Blandecques, a village near St Omer, in which the English Jesuits of St Omer's College, the ancestor of Stonyhurst, had a country house for the boys' summer holidays). The scholastics were encouraged, too, to take more interest in the world outside than they were as novices. One medium for this was the newly founded 'English Academy', which heard papers from the scholastics and held debates, often on topical subjects. In his third year Hopkins read a paper, 'Thoughts on Mobs'.

Hopkins had his own consolations for the exactingness of the course. The wild Lancashire countryside excited him: later, when he returned to Stonyhurst, he wrote to Bridges of the 'noble view of this Lancashire landscape, Pendle Hill, Ribblesdale, the fells, and all round, bleakish but solemn and beautiful'. He discovered Duns

Scotus in the Stonyhurst library. And his Journal records more and more instances of his. delight in inscapes, in trees, flowers, clouds, buildings; even the severe winter of 1869 gave him the chance to observe and record the strange and beautiful effects of the hard frost. Nevertheless, his health gave some concern. He was again not allowed to fast in Lent; and on hurrying back to Stonyhurst on foot too quickly after his last August holiday, he records vividly an ominous experience: 'In fact being unwell I was quite downcast: nature in all her parcels and faculties gaped and fell apart, *fatiscebat*, like a clod cleaving and holding only by strings of root. But this must often be.' There was too a repetition of the outbreak of sobbing he had given way to at Roehampton. The reading this time was of the decision of the formerly rich and worldly Abbot de Rancé to become a monk in 1663: an experience that clearly moved Hopkins very greatly:

> After a time of trial and especially a morning in which I did not know which way to turn as the account of De Rancé's final conversion was being read at dinner the verse *Qui confidunt in Domino sicut mons Sion* which satisfied him and resolved him to enter his abbey of La Trappe by the mercy of God came strongly home to me too, so that I was choked for a little while and could not keep in my tears.

Hopkins's three years training in philosophy ended in late August 1873. On the 28th he was ordered to return to Roehampton as Professor of Rhetoric, to teach the twenty-three Juniors who had completed the novitiate, and five novices, Classics and English Literature. It was not a particularly exacting task, and to his mother Hopkins wrote that 'the year's teaching was given as a rest'. The importance to his own later poetry of the 'Lecture Notes: Rhetoric' he wrote during this year, including notes on 'Poetry and Verse', will be stressed later (see pp. 68–9). To some extent, the year's teaching was a respite from his own strict Jesuit training. That continued at the end of the following August, when he went to St Beuno's College, North Wales, for three years' study in theology.

The college of theology: St Beuno's, North Wales, 1874–7

Hopkins arrived at St Beuno's, near St Asaph, for three years' study of theology (rather than four, as he had expected) on 28 August 1874. Although his Journal ends at the following February, there are sufficient entries to show how deeply affected he was by the North Welsh countryside. He was, as always, particularly sensitive to colours: to the 'beautiful liquid cast of blue' of the landscape and the 'many-coloured smokes in the valley'. On 12 October, he noted, 'The sky was iron grey and the valley, full of Welsh charm and graceful sadness, all in grave colours lay like a painted napkin.' To his mother he wrote that when he saw Snowdon and the neighbouring mountains, with the clouds lifting, 'it gives me a rise of the heart'. If he was as ready to be emotionally moved as at Roehampton or Stonyhurst, he seems to have been more in control of his feelings, and happier. At the first ordination of priests he witnessed, he was, he recorded, 'by God's mercy deeply touched' at the singing of the *Veni Creator* and the giving of the Orders. After his first bathe in St Winefred's well nearby, with its stories of miraculous cures,

> The strong unfailing flow of the water and the chain of cures from year to year all these centuries, [he wrote] took hold of my mind with wonder at the bounty of God in one of His saints . . . even now the stress and buoyancy and abundance of the water is before my eyes.

This new mood of near-elation obviously played its part in the wonderful flowering of his poetry in *The Wreck of the Deutschland*, written at the turn of 1875–76, and the sonnets that followed it in 1877, his final year at St Beuno's.

Meanwhile, Hopkins needed all his own buoyancy to struggle with a subject that was entirely new to him. R.F. Clarke, who joined Hopkins at St Beuno's, thus describes the studies in theology:

> Here the work is certainly hard, especially during the first two years. On three days in the week, the student who has passed successfully through his philosophical course has to attend two lectures in the morning and three in the afternoon. The morning lectures are on moral and dogmatic theology; and those in the afternoon on canon law or history, dogmatic theology, and Hebrew, the last for half an hour only. Besides this, on each of these afternoons there is held a circle or disputation such as I have described above. . . . In addition to these constant disputations there is held every three months a more solemn assembly of the same kind, at which the whole house is present and the rector presides, in which two of the students are chosen to defend for an hour continuously a number of theses against the attacks of all comers, the professors themselves included.
>
> During the third and fourth years of the course of theology, lectures in Scripture are substituted for those on moral theology and Hebrew. At the end of the third year the young Jesuit (if a man of thirty-four or thirty-five can be accounted young) is ordained priest, and during his last year his lectures are fewer, and he has privately to prepare himself for a general examination in theology, on which depends in great measure whether he has the grade of a professed father in the Society or the lower degree of what is called a 'spiritual coadjutor'.

In addition to the lectures and 'circle', a 'case of conscience'—
a hypothetical ethical problem—was prepared by three of the
theologians in turn weekly and discussed.

The theology taught had not changed substantially since that
studied at Liège during the penal days. It was Thomism as interpreted by the Jesuit theologian Suarez, of whom Hopkins later wrote
to Dixon: 'He is a man of vast volume of mind, but without originality
or brilliancy; he treats everything satisfactorily, but you never remember a phrase of his, the manner is nothing.' Hopkins was writing
with approval, to illustrate that 'brilliancy does not suit us'. Two
Jesuit theologians, Joseph Crehan and George Tyrrell, who taught
theology later at St Beuno's, were considerably more critical. Hopkins
himself confessed that he found the course exacting, as he had found
the philosophy course: 'The close pressure of my theological studies
leaves me time for hardly anything', he told Bridges; 'the course is
very hard, it must be said.'

Everyday life for the thirty-five to forty theologians was outwardly
uneventful. There were regular debates and papers read to an Essay
Society; for recreation, walks in the Welsh hills (the early ones
vividly recorded in Hopkins's Journal), skating, fishing, climbing
and musical entertainments. Annual holidays were taken on the
Welsh coast. A retreat at the start of the course was followed by the
tonsure and the four minor orders ('Doorkeepers, Readers, Exorcists,
and Acolytes: their use is almost obsolete', Hopkins explained to his
mother). The theologians preached sermons in the refectory (one of
Hopkins's, comparing the Sea of Galilee with the Vale of Clwyd,
was found extremely funny: 'People laughed at it prodigiously, I saw
some of them roll on their chairs with laughter', he recorded). In
his second year Hopkins was appointed 'Beadle of the Moral Theology
School'—that is, chief of that year's theologians.

St Beuno's was notoriously cold, with a quite inadequate central-
heating system; but Hopkins seems to have stood up to it. It was
preparing for examinations in his final year that took some toll. In
March, before his examination in moral theology to hear confessions,
he wrote to his mother: 'Going over moral theology over and over
again and in a hurry is the most wearisome work and tonight at all
events I am so tired I am good for nothing.' He passed the examination, but in April wrote to Bridges: 'I am very, very tired, yes "a
thousand times and yet a thousand times" and "scarce can go or
creep".' That month he was sent for his health to Rhyl, on the sea,
for a few days. In July 1877 he passed his final examination, and,
after a retreat, was with fifteen others ordained priest (following the
other orders of subdeacon and deacon) on 22 September.

Hopkins expected, as several letters make clear, to be promoted

St Beuno's College, North Wales

to a further year of theological studies. Success in a general examination in theology at the end of it would have given him the chance of becoming a Professed Father, with chances of higher academic preferment in the Society, instead of, as he became, a Spiritual Coadjutor. But in October he was appointed instead to teach at Mount St Mary's College, Chesterfield, Derbyshire. His health and propensity to fatigue at St Beuno's may have worried his superiors; the suggestion that his Scotism got him into difficulties with them has already been mentioned. There is no firm evidence as to why he was not promoted to a further year. But there can be no doubt that he soon keenly missed St Beuno's itself and its surroundings. In a letter to his father, on returning after a holiday with his family in August 1877, he wrote: 'No sooner were we among the Welsh hills than I saw the hawks flying, and other pleasant sights soon to be seen no more.' Of what took its place at Mount St Mary's, he wrote to Bridges the following February: 'Life here is as dank as ditch-water'; and, in April, 'My muse turned utterly sullen in the Sheffield smoke-ridden air'.

The tertianship: Roehampton, 1881–2

After four busy and often disheartening years as a priest in parishes that included Liverpool and Glasgow slums, Hopkins returned to Manresa House in October 1881, for his 'tertianship', the third year as a novice that the Jesuit spends before taking his last vows. It is intended as a year of renewal. The daily routine, both spiritual and domestic, was much the same as that of the novitiate; its most important event was, again, the Long Retreat of thirty days, which began on 7 November. Hopkins kept full notes of it: they comprise, in fact, the central section of his devotional writings published by Fr Christopher Devlin. As Devlin points out, their central inspiration —deriving from meditations on the *Spiritual Exercises*—was 'the great sacrifice', Christ's crucifixion.

There were only nine tertians, under the tertian master, Fr Robert Whitty, out of a total community of 100. Their rules were strict. They saw no newspapers nor read any but spiritual books; they could not leave the grounds without a permit; they could not speak to the Juniors nor novices. In Lent they went out to give retreats and help with other mission duties. In a long letter to Dixon, who mistakenly believed that a tertian could still withdraw from his vows, Hopkins explained the purpose of the tertianship:

> I see you do not understand my position in the Society. This Tertianship or Third Year of Probation or second Noviceship, for it is variously called in the Institute, is not really a noviceship at all in the sense of a time during which a candidate or probationer

Hopkins in 1880

51

makes trial of our life and is free to withdraw. At the end of the noviceship proper we take vows which are perpetually binding and renew them every six months (not *for* every six months but for life) till we are professed or take the final degree we are to hold, of which in the Society there are several. It is in preparation for these last vows that we make the tertianship; which is called a *schola affectus* and is meant to enable us to recover that fervour which may have cooled through application to study and contact with the world. Its exercises are however nearly the same as those of the first noviceship.

He went on to give his own attitude to his vocation:

As for myself, I have not only made my vows publicly some two and twenty times but I make them to myself every day, so that I should be black with perjury if I drew back now. And beyond that I can say with St Peter: To whom shall I go? *Tu verba vitae aeternae habes.* Besides all which, my mind is here more at peace than it has ever been and I would gladly live all my life, if it were so to be, in as great or a greater seclusion from the world and be busied only with God. But in the midst of outward occupations not only the mind is drawn away from God, which may be at the call of duty and be God's will, but unhappily the will too is entangled, worldly interests freshen, and worldly ambitions revive. The man who in the world is as dead to the world as if he were buried in the cloister is already a saint. But this is our ideal.

The tertians were given three 'repose days' during their Long Retreat; and were allowed visitors on days of recreation (on one of them Bridges came to see Hopkins). Hopkins clearly felt greatly refreshed by the year. He told Bridges: 'It is ... a great rest to be here and I am in a very contented frame of mind,' and later: 'the calm of mind is delightful: I am afraid I shall leave it behind.' Though in that last letter he said he found the life 'trying—weakening, I mean', there are no complaints about his health. The sense of renewal also encouraged his creative hopes. Besides a projected poetic drama on St Winefred and the 'great ode' he hoped to write on Edmund Campion, he was planning a Commentary on the *Spiritual Exercises* (he wrote sixteen pages of a draft of it during his last week), a treatise on the idea of sacrifice in ancient religions, and a book on Greek lyric art. But none was ever finished: they were, no doubt, among what he, more than four years later, described to Baillie as 'beginnings of things, ever so many, which it seems to me might well have been done, ruins and wrecks'.

In January and June the tertians renewed their vows; and on 15 August 1882, the Feast of the Assumption, they took their final vows, Hopkins and four others taking those of Spiritual Coadjutors.

From the end of his tertianship until his death in 1889 Hopkins taught Classics: for eighteen months to the Jesuit 'Philosophers' at Stonyhurst; from February 1884 at University College, Dublin, then under the control of the Jesuits. Hopkins's appointments were as Fellow of the newly established Royal University of Ireland and as Professor of Greek at University College, one of its constituent Colleges. His testimonials for the Professorship included one from Jowett of Balliol. There was a strongly supported local candidate; and, as Hopkins told Bridges, 'There was an Irish row over my election.'

Despite his high-sounding titles and apparent academic recognition, Hopkins's main tasks were to conduct six examinations a year, of up to 500 candidates a time, and to take classes in Latin and Greek. For a man of his weak health and intense scrupulosity, the load of examining was crushing. It caused him severe eye-strain and drove him at times to near-prostration. It is a constant complaint in his letters: '331 accounts of the First Punic War with trimmings', he wrote to Bridges in October 1886, 'have sweated me down to nearer my lees and usual alluvial low water mudflats, groans, despair, and yearnings.' What records there are suggest that his lecturing was well over the heads of most of his pupils.

Hopkins's teaching appointments were clearly intended to be congenial to a scholar. When he went to Stonyhurst, the Provincial had encouraged him to continue his writing. The members of the small Jesuit community at University College, where he lived, were cultivated and learned and Hopkins liked living among them. The President, Fr Delaney, he described to his mother as being 'as generous, cheering, and open-hearted a man as I ever lived with'. He became a close friend of Fr Robert Curtis, Professor of Natural Science ('my comfort beyond what I can say and a kind of godsend I never expected to have'), and spent walking holidays with him in North Wales and Scotland. Another colleague was Thomas Arnold (Matthew Arnold's brother), an early Oxford convert, now Professor of English, for whose *Manual of English Literature* Hopkins wrote a note on R.W. Dixon's poetry. He saw much of Fr Matthew Russell, editor of the *Irish Monthly*, which published two of his Latin versions of Shakespeare's songs. Through Russell he met W.B. Yeats's father, the artist John Butler Yeats, and, on one occasion at least, W.B. Yeats himself, and the poet Katharine Tynan. Yeats's early verse contributions to the *Dublin University Review*, 1885–86, he found 'striking', but *Mosada*—which Yeats's father gave him—he could not 'think highly of'. Many years later W.B. Yeats remembered Hopkins as a 'querulous, sensitive scholar'; and Katharine Tynan described him as 'small and childish-looking, yet like a child-sage, nervous too and very sensitive, with a small ivory-pale face'. Between his lecturing and examining duties, Hopkins was given quite frequent holidays, some of them spent with his family; and in Ireland he was befriended by an elderly lady, Miss Cassidy, of Monasterevan, Kildare, with whom he often stayed: 'one of the props and struts of my existence', he described her to Bridges.

Outwardly, then, Hopkins may not seem to have been particularly isolated or desolate during these five years in Dublin. But his letters (particularly to Bridges), Retreat notes and poems—above all, the six so-called 'terrible sonnets' of 1885—tell a very different story. Two months after his arrival, he wrote to Bridges of 'recovering from a deep fit of nervous prostration'; and, a year later, to Baillie, of his constitutional melancholy becoming 'more distributed, constant, and crippling . . . when I am at the worst, though my judgment is never affected, my state is much like madness.' That year, 1885, his sense of desolation was at its most acute. He felt utterly isolated; deserted by God; and convinced that his creative powers, which might have saved him, were dead. That September he wrote to Bridges: 'If I could but produce work I should not mind its being buried, silenced, and going no further; but it kills me to be times eunuch and never to beget.' That image of the eunuch ends one of his final poems, *Thou art indeed just, Lord*, and comes in a late Retreat note. Yet in that same letter he promised Bridges 'five or more' sonnets, four of which 'came like inspirations unbidden and against my will'; in the previous May he told him he had written two sonnets: 'If ever anything was written in blood one of these was'. Bridges thought the sonnet 'written in blood' was *Carrion Comfort*; it may equally have been *No worst, there is none*, written on the same MS page. There can be little doubt that the 'five or more' sonnets— never in fact sent to Bridges—were the 'terrible sonnets' (Nos 64–69 in Hopkins's *Poems*, fourth edition).

Many factors clearly played their part in bringing about Hopkins's feeling of desolation in Dublin: bad health (the nervous depression he was continually subject to obviously worsened), the burden of examining, his sense of being an exile. The political situation undoubtedly exacerbated the last of these. As an ultra-patriotic Englishman, he detested Irish nationalism; but many of the Irish Catholic bishops were fervent nationalists. 'One archbishop backs robbery, the other rebellion,' he wrote to Bridges in 1887; 'the people in good faith believe and will follow them.' To his mother he had written in 1885: 'The grief of mind I go through over politics, over what I read and hear and see in Ireland about Ireland and about England, is such that I can neither express it nor bear to speak of it.' His conviction that, as a Catholic in Ireland, he was unwillingly supporting rebellion, is made clear in a striking image in one of his

University College, Dublin

final Retreat notes: 'Against my will my pains, laborious and distasteful, like prisoners made to serve the enemies' gunners, go to help on this cause.' The situation at University College was itself depressing: his colleagues may have been congenial enough; but the dilapidation and bareness of the College made life 'like living at a temporary Junction'.

There were no doubt less conscious reasons for Hopkins's crippling sense of desolation. Some have found its source in an unconscious conflict between priest and poet; others in the suppression of passionate, possibly homosexual, feelings. Catholic writers have stressed that spiritual 'aridity' is an experience fully prepared for, as part of a Jesuit's life of sacrifice, in the *Spiritual Exercises*. The most convincing explanation—in so far as there can be a single explanation —seems to be that put forward by Fr Christopher Devlin in *Sermons and Devotional Writings* (Oxford, 1959): that, in his scrupulous search for personal holiness, Hopkins exaggerated the distinction between his 'affective will', his love of beauty, and his 'elective will', his desire for sanctity.

Hopkins may have felt that his creative powers were dead; but the 'terrible sonnets' were followed, over the next four years, by nine more poems, showing a variety of moods: they include *Harry Ploughman*, *That Nature is a Heraclitean Fire and of the Comfort of the Resurrection*, the unfinished *Epithalamion*, written for his brother Everard's wedding, and his last sonnet, *To R.B.*, written six weeks before his death and addressed to Bridges. And these last Dublin years witnessed in him a remarkable amount of other intellectual activity. In succession, he worked on a projected book on Homer; carried on a long and scholarly correspondence with his friend Alexander Baillie about possible early relations between Egypt and Greece; and began another book on 'the Dorian Measure or on Rhythm in general'. Such varied activity undoubtedly answered a need; but, sadly, none of it was finished and virtually nothing of it remains. In addition, he spent a great deal of time composing music (he sent his compositions to Sir Robert Stewart, Professor of Music at Trinity College, Dublin, and was clearly put out by some of his criticism); and in 1888 he took up drawing again.

In spring 1889 Hopkins's old Oxford friend, Baron Francis de Paravicini, Tutor of Balliol, visited him. As de Paravicini's wife wrote to Mrs Hopkins later, he 'thought him looking very ill then, and said that he was much depressed'. The de Paravicinis were sufficiently worried to take what steps they could to have him sent back to England; but it was too late. Hopkins contracted typhoid fever in early May and, after a month's illness, died on 8 June. According to his first biographer, Fr G.F. Lahey, his last words were 'I am so happy, I am so happy'.

3 Literary background

Ruskin, the Pre-Raphaelites and Pater

On 10 July 1863 Hopkins wrote to his friend Alexander Baillie from the Isle of Wight: 'I am sketching (in pencil chiefly) a good deal. I venture to hope you will approve of some of the sketches in a Ruskinese point of view:—if you do not, who will, my sole congenial thinker on art?'

In *All My Eyes See* (pp. 64–67) Norman White put together four of Hopkins's drawings (two of them done on this Isle of Wight holiday) with four of Ruskin's on similar subjects from nature; and Ruskin's immense influence is at once dramatically clear. How strong it was in choice of subject too the letter to Baillie also reveals quite clearly:

> There are the most deliciously graceful Giottesque ashes (should one say *ashs*?) here—I do not mean Giottesque though, Peruginesque, Fra-Angelical (!), in Raphael's earlier manner. I think I have told you that I have particular periods of admiration for particular things in Nature; for a certain time I am astonished at the beauty of a tree, shape, effect etc., then when the passion, so to speak, has subsided, it is consigned to my treasury of explored beauty and acknowledged with admiration and interest ever after, while something new takes its place in my enthusiasm. The present fury is the ash, and perhaps barley and two shapes of growth in leaves and one in tree boughs and also a conformation of fine-weather cloud.

Almost everything that Hopkins created and recorded in the first surges of his enthusiasm at Oxford owed something to Ruskin: the drawings of natural objects to *Modern Painters* (he reminded himself to read it in 1865, but had certainly read Vol. I by then); the numerous medieval architectural drawings to *Seven Lamps of Architecture* (after his first drawing in 1863, he cited Ruskin's admiration for the superior beauty of Gothic over all other schools); the 'innocence of eye' that he brought then and throughout his life to all his observation of nature, to *The Elements of Drawing*. But Ruskin's influence went far beyond Hopkins's sketches. The sensuousness of his early verse—which, when he abandoned poetry for seven years, went into his Journal—clearly owed a debt to Ruskin as well as, more obviously, to Keats; as, indeed, did his whole way of looking at things. Hopkins's urge throughout his poetry to explain, to communicate and to praise: all these Ruskin had stressed as the artist's duties. Above all, the artist should express both the infinite variety of Nature's details *and* her wholeness.

This insisted-on allegiance to both fact and vision played a great part in Hopkins's search for an aesthetic. In his longest undergraduate Essay, 'On the Origin of Beauty: A Platonic Dialogue', 1865, the central figure, the newly elected Oxford Professor of Aesthetics, is clearly Ruskinian (Ruskin was in fact the first holder of the Slade Chair of Fine Art at Oxford four years later). The Professor's first example, to establish scientific criteria of beauty as against purely subjective criteria, was the horse-chestnut fan, followed by oak and chestnut trees. The horse-chestnut was one of Ruskin's favourite trees; but more important was his constant search for Nature's 'laws' (the following year we find Hopkins noting: 'I have now found the law of the oak leaves'). In a further Essay, 'The Probable Future of Metaphysics', written in 1867, Hopkins went further than Ruskin in his search for absolute beauty. He now posited an ideal Platonic form behind every form in nature. But the descriptions of his walking tour of Switzerland the following summer are, as Norman White has pointed out (*All My Eyes See*, p. 64), the most Ruskinian of Hopkins's Journal notes: they often describe the same mountains, glaciers and waterfalls that Ruskin had described in his Diary of 1835. They show that, however philosophically buttressed Hopkins's aesthetic might now be, Ruskin's vision was still very much alive in it.

In 'On the Origin of Beauty', the fictional sketcher, Middleton, is represented as one of the Pre-Raphaelite painters who had decorated the Oxford Union with frescoes in 1857. The Pre-Raphaelites (the original 'Brotherhood' were D.G. Rossetti, Holman Hunt and Millais) admired Ruskin intensely and Ruskin looked to them as the leaders of a more 'real' school of art. Not surprisingly, they were one of Hopkins's earliest enthusiasms. In the letter to Baillie of 10 July 1863, already quoted, Hopkins described Millais's *Eve of St Agnes*, which he had just seen, as 'the conception of her by a genius', and continued: 'Those three pictures by Millais in this year's Academy have opened my eyes. I see that he is the greatest English painter, one of the greatest of the world.' Millais, he went on, represented 'the greatest perfection' of the Pre-Raphaelite school, and the school itself was 'at last arriving at Nature's self'.

The following July he had, he wrote to Baillie, 'great things to tell'. He had met Christina Rossetti and Holman Hunt at his friends the Gurneys. It was no doubt this introduction which fired a spate of queries and comments on the Pre-Raphaelites and other medieval schools of painting in his diary the same month: 'To ask ... about

Winter Fuel *by John Everett Millais. Hopkins gives a detailed criticism of it in his* Journal. *He greatly admired Millais.*

the Preraphaelite Brotherhood, the French Preraphaelites, the Düsseldorf school etc.' It was clearly their medievalism which primarily interested him, rather than their dedication to natural detail. He noted the names of two of the founders of the 'Nazarenes', the German religious painters who had formed a kind of Pre-Raphaelite brotherhood in Rome in 1810–11; then that of Baron Henri Leys, the leading Belgian mid-century medievalist; with, finally, a disappointed comment on the Belgian school: 'Sort of French Preraphaelitism, but very little medievalism *in feeling* though medieval subjects.'

It was this same month that he wrote *A Voice from the World*, an answer to Christina Rossetti's *Convent Threshold*; and he continued to admire her poetry—more, in fact, than that of her more acclaimed brother, Dante Gabriel Rossetti. But Hopkins's committed enthusiasm for the Pre-Raphaelites only lasted as long as his serious ambition to become a painter. Thereafter their influence on his poetry was minimal; and, on his aesthetic vision, absorbed in that of Ruskin. But he still saw their paintings whenever he could and made detailed comments on them.

Much the most interesting of Hopkins's Oxford tutors, from the point of view of his aesthetic development, was Walter Pater. Pater was less than four years older than Hopkins; he had become a Fellow of Brasenose in 1864. Hopkins was his pupil in the Easter Term of 1866. How much influence Pater had over him it is very difficult to say. It is tempting to find his influence in Hopkins's long Essay, 'On the Origin of Beauty: A Platonic Dialogue', already referred to; but that is dated 12 May 1865, a year before Pater probably taught him; it is much too long for a weekly essay, and was more probably written for the Hexameron, the High Church essay society to which Hopkins belonged. In fact, the two men's positions were very different. Pater was already moving towards the aim he declared for himself in his 'Essay on Winckelmann' (January 1867), 'to attain the knowledge of beauty' as the supreme end of life; in the famous 'Conclusion' to *The Renaissance* (1873) this aim could only be accomplished through art. Only art could give 'the highest quality to your moments as they pass, and simply for those moments' sake'. Beauty or art as an end in itself—as a bulwark against life's transience—was never Hopkins's creed. It always revealed for him a Higher Being, God. 'On the Origin of Beauty' is a beautifully handled, provocative enquiry into why we find things beautiful, of great interest in the development of Hopkins's perception; but it was not intended to go beyond that. At the same time, Hopkins clearly found Pater very sympathetic. Humphry Ward wrote of Pater's early teaching at Brasenose: 'No man demanded more clear and accurate thinking, or a more exact expression of it in words.' To this Hopkins would certainly have responded. More surprisingly, he does not seem to have been repelled by Pater's rejection of Christianity. After their first evening walk together, in April 1866, he described him in a line from one of Charles Tennyson Turner's sonnets: 'Bleak-faced Neology in cap and gown'; the tone is more amused than upset. A month later he simply records, without comment: 'Pater talking two hours against Xtianity.' The following June, after his conversion, he lunched with Pater in London and, with him, met the painter Simeon Solomon. Eleven years later he was pleased and flattered to hear from Bridges that Pater remembered and took an interest in him. When he returned to Oxford in 1878 as a priest, Pater, he wrote, was 'one of the men I saw most of'.

Inscape and instress

Hopkins first uses these two terms he coined in some notes on the early Greek philosopher Parmenides, probably made in February 1868. 'Instress' comes first: 'His great text . . . means that all things are upheld by instress and are meaningless without it.' Then comes: 'His feeling for instress, for the flush and foredrawn, and for inscape/ is most striking and from this one can understand Plato's reverence for him as the great father of Realism.' The reference to Plato is important: it is probably as near as we can get to an origin for both terms. Hopkins had long been seeking a metaphysical explanation for the hold on the mind—the excitement—that certain forms and patterns in nature exert on us. It is the subject of his essay, 'On the Origin of Beauty', 1865; and pursued again in a later one, 'The Probable Future of Metaphysics', 1867, where Platonism is offered as the only alternative to 'a philosophy of flux'.

There seems little doubt, therefore, that both concepts to some extent point to Plato's 'Ideal Forms'; beyond that, they could foreshadow the 'Divine harmony' which such Forms ultimately revealed. From the beginning, then, the use of both 'inscape' and 'instress' has, for Hopkins, the excitement of philosophical as well as aesthetic discovery. 'Inscape' he uses to describe the beauty of pattern which expresses a thing's inner or essential form; or, as he put it in a *Journal* entry, 'the immediate scape of the thing, which unmistakeably distinguishes and individualises things', the quality which gives it its selfhood. 'Instress' he uses in two senses: (1) the energy or stress that 'upholds' an object's inscape, that gives it its being (as in the note on Parmenides, above); and (2) the force which the inscape exerts on the mind or feelings of the perceiver. Often these two senses merge. In the best-known of all his uses of 'instress' (in Stanza 5 of *The Wreck of the Deutschland*) he uses it as a verb:

> Since, tho' he is under the world's splendour and wonder,
> His mystery must be instressed, stressed.

The force of God's mystery must be impressed upon our being, 'come to stress' in us.

A few months after the notes on Parmenides come the first uses of both words in his *Journal*. 'Instress' again comes first, on a visit to the National Gallery (27 June 1868): 'Query has not Giotto the instress of loveliness?' Two weeks later, on his walking tour in Switzerland, we have 'inscape', here as a verb: 'Swiss trees are, like English, well inscaped—in quains [coigns, wedge-shaped blocks]' (7 July 1868). From then on, both words are used for a multitude of objects. Trees predominate, as we would expect from his love of them shown in poems and sketches; before his coinages, he had recorded: 'I have now found the law of the oak leaves. It is of platter-shaped stars altogether' (Journal, 19 July 1866). But almost all the other objects or aspects of nature that excited him are recorded in terms of their inscape or instress: rushing water, glaciers, clouds, sunsets, skies, stars, mountains, flowers. Presence or absence of inscape (or instress) becomes the main criterion for judging pictures and buildings: Briton Rivière's *Apollo* has it; Millais's *Scotch Firs* is lessened by its absence; Ely Cathedral is remarkable for 'the all-powerfulness of instress in mode'.

In all these examples there is a strong tincture of the ideal; in a Journal entry of May 1870 an inscape explicitly foreshadows the divine: 'I do not think I have ever seen anything more beautiful than the bluebell I have been looking at. I know the beauty of our Lord by it. Its inscape is mixed of strength and grace.' From now on, Hopkins clearly identifies the word with a beauty—or reality —which alone gives things meaning. 'All the world is full of inscape', he writes in one Journal entry; and, in March 1871: 'Unless you refresh the mind from time to time you cannot always remember or believe how deep the inscape in things is.' After admiring the beams of a great barn, he records, 'I thought how sadly beauty of inscape was unknown and buried away from simple people and yet how near at hand it was if they had eyes to see it and it could be called out everywhere again' (July 1872); and, on the felling of an ash tree: 'There came at that moment a great pang and I wished to die and not to see the inscapes of the world destroyed any more' (April 1873).

For Hopkins the poet, his last recorded use of the word is the most interesting. On 15 February 1879, he writes to Bridges, defending his poetry from the charge of oddness:

As air, melody, is what strikes me most of all in music and design in painting, so design, pattern, or what I am in the habit of calling 'inscape' is what I above all aim at in poetry. Now it is the virtue of design, pattern, or inscape to be distinctive and it is the vice of distinctiveness to become queer. This vice I cannot have inscaped.

Not only does his poetry aim at distilling the distinctiveness of things, but the individual poem itself is a distinctive pattern, an inscape of sound and shape and structure, as well as of meaning.

Hopkins and nineteenth-century poetry

Hopkins's earliest poetry shows how readily and excitedly he absorbed the young Keats. *A Vision of the Mermaids*, dated Christmas 1862, a few months before he left Highgate for Oxford, emulates Keats at his most sensuous, especially in its fascination with colour. The colours are strong, violent, the enrichment of a fantasy-world:—

> Plum-purple was the west; but spikes of light
> Spear'd open lustrous gashes, crimson-white.

And, of the mermaids themselves:

> clouds of violet glow'd
> On prankèd scale; or threads of carmine, shot
> Thro' silver, gloom'd to a blood-vivid clot.

Four years later, in *The Habit of Perfection*, this sheer enjoyment in sensation has been replaced by its opposite, an equally strong impulse towards asceticism; but the images that evoke the senses to be denied still owe a great deal to Keats:

> Palate, the hutch of tasty lust,
> Desire not to be rinsed with wine:
> . . .
> O feel-of-primrose hands, O feet
> That want the yield of plushy sward . . .

When Hopkins returned to writing poetry with *The Wreck of the Deutschland*, Keats's direct influence had clearly gone; but not Hopkins's admiration for him. Likeness to Keats ('imagery inheriting Keats's mantle; the other-world of imagination') was the highest praise he could give to Dixon's poems; and two of his last letters to Patmore, who had classed Keats as a 'feminine genius' and 'unlikest of our poets to Shakespere', include some of the most perceptive and sympathetic criticism of Keats that had then been written: the more interesting for what it surely implies of Hopkins's attitude to his own poetry and poetic development. This is from the second of them (6 May 1888):

[Keats's] mind had, as it seems to me, the distinctively masculine powers in abundance, his character the manly virtues, but while he gave himself up to dreaming and self indulgence of course they were in abeyance. Nor do I mean that he would have turned to a life of virtue—only God can know that—, but that his genius would have taken to an austerer utterance in art. Reason, thought, what he did not want to live by, would have asserted itself presently and perhaps have been as much more powerful than that of his contemporaries as his sensibility or impressionableness, by which he did want to live, was keener and richer than theirs.

Most of the poems that Hopkins wrote as an Oxford undergraduate express religious doubt and uncertainty; and few of them go far outside accepted Victorian poetic modes for such expression. Some are clearly imitative: *A Voice from the World* of Christina Rossetti (it was written as an answer to her *Convent Threshold*); some stanzas of *Nondum* (written in 1866, the year of his conversion) of Newman's *Lead, Kindly Light*; his fragmentary pastoral, *Richard*, of Arnold's *The Scholar Gipsy*. *The Lover's Stars* he described as 'a trifle in something like Coventry Patmore's style'. Much more interesting, as a pointer to Hopkins's later and true originality, is the long letter of September 1864 he wrote to his friend Baillie on what he called the 'Parnassian' in poetry. 'Parnassian' is secondary to 'poetry proper, the language of inspiration'.

> It can only be spoken by poets, but it is not in the highest sense poetry. . . . It is spoken *on and from the level* of a poet's mind, not, as in the other case, when the inspiration which is the gift of genius, raises him above himself. . . . In a poet's particular kind of Parnassian lies most of his style, of his manner, of his mannerism if you like. . . . I believe that when a poet palls on us it is because of his Parnassian. We seem to have found out his secret.

The chief impetus to the letter was the 'Parnassian' in Tennyson, for whom he had expressed much early admiration ('a horrible thing has happened to me. I have begun to *doubt* Tennyson'). But 'no author palls so much as Wordsworth; this is because he writes such an "intolerable deal of" Parnassian'. Truly inspired, both poets moved him deeply. Stanza 121 of Tennyson's *In Memoriam*, beginning 'Sad Hesper o'er the buried sun,' is 'divine, terribly beautiful'. From Wordsworth's Ode, *Intimations of Immortality*, human nature 'got a shock', believed Wordsworth had seen something denied to other men, 'and the tremble from it is spreading. . . . I am, ever since I knew the ode, in that tremble.'

The true criterion of genuine poetry, even in 1864, is inspiration, 'a mood of great, abnormal in fact, mental acuteness'. If this was so for other poets, even more true did it become for his own work. Hopkins's most rigorous demands were always made on himself. Such inspiration is a long way from either the 'oddity' with which Bridges charged him in the Preface to his edition of his friend's poems, or the '*too* manifest . . . system and learned theory' which Patmore found in him. It also makes clear that the distinctive design or 'inscape' that Hopkins aimed at in his poetry was something much more deeply felt and 'true' than the individual or idiosyncratic style of most of his contemporaries. With them he shows his impatience. 'What fun if you were a classic!', he writes to Bridges. 'So few people have style, except individual style or manner—not Tennyson nor Swinburne nor Morris, not to name the scarecrow misbegotten Browning crew'; and he adds, to pour salt in the wound: 'The Brownings are very fine too in their ghastly way.'

Hopkins was especially sensitive to superficial resemblances between contemporary poets' innovations and his own. Browning's use of everyday language and of speech rhythms was a case in point. Hopkins had to admire its force, for it apparently chimed in with his own; but Browning's approach to both life and poetry he thoroughly disliked, and any parallel drawn with his was clearly anathema. He makes his attitude clear in a sharp comment to Bridges: 'I always think however that your mind towards my verse is like mine towards Browning's: I greatly admire the touches and the details, but the general effect, the whole, offends me, I think it repulsive.' What he really disliked in Browning comes out in a letter to Dixon:

> Browning has, I think, many frigidities. Any untruth to nature, to human nature, is frigid. Now he has got a great deal of what came in with Kingsley and the Broad Church school, a way of talking (and making his people talk) with the air and spirit of a man bouncing up from table with his mouth full of bread and cheese and saying that he meant to stand no blasted nonsense. . . . The effect of this style is a frigid bluster. . . . Indeed I hold with the oldfashioned criticism that Browning is not really a poet, that he has all the gifts but the one needful and the pearls without the string.

Walt Whitman was another case, and clearly a more embarrassing one: for, as Hopkins confessed to Bridges in October 1882, 'I always knew in my heart Walt Whitman's mind to be more like my own than any other man's living. As he is a very great scoundrel this is not a pleasant confession.' Hopkins's letter—his 'de-Whitmaniser', he called it—was a reply to Bridges's suggestion that *The Leaden Echo and the Golden Echo* had been influenced by Whitman, whose *Leaves of Grass* had been published eight years before. Hopkins pointed out that he had only read 'half a dozen pieces at most' of Whitman and that his poem owed nothing to him. It is an important letter because he then goes on to distingusih between Whitman's use of long lines and irregular rhythms and his own. Whitman's poems were in 'an irregular rhythmic prose'; his own poem, on the contrary, was 'very highly wrought. The long lines are not rhythm run to seed: everything is weighed and timed in them.' For Hopkins, highly elaborated and disciplined experiments in rhythm were of the very essence of his mature poetry: it was vital to show that, whatever apparent resemblance they might have, they lay at the opposite pole from a rhythm—as Hopkins put it—'in its last ruggedness and decomposition into common prose'. Hopkins was sensitive enough on the subject, when he sent Bridges *Harry Ploughman* five years later, to ask him to let him know 'if there is anything like it in Walt Whitman, as perhaps there may be, and I should be sorry for that'.

Towards another innovator in rhythm, Swinburne, Hopkins's attitude was more complicated. Swinburne was already something of a hero to Oxford lovers of poetry when Hopkins was an undergraduate. He had gone down from Balliol a few years before, in 1859, having somewhat surprisingly already become a close friend of Jowett. He knew D.G. Rossetti intimately and was much admired by the Pre-Raphaelites. Hopkins records seeing him when he returned to Oxford to take his degree in May 1868. Before this he had made his moral disapproval clear in a letter to Baillie: 'I mean for instance that it is impossible not personally to form an opinion against the morality of a writer like Swinburne'; and Swinburne's outspoken hostility to religion could only alienate him further. By 1877 Hopkins could refer laconically to him, to Bridges, as a 'plague of mankind'. But as a poet and innovator he knew Swinburne had to be reckoned with; or, rather, he knew he had to discriminate—and make clear to himself, as well as to Bridges and Dixon—between what was valuable in Swinburne and what was not. The resulting critical comments are doubly interesting, in that they tell us as much about Hopkins's own attitude to poetry and poetic innovation as they do about Swinburne himself.

'Swinburne is a strange phenomenon', Hopkins wrote to Dixon in December 1881, 'his poetry seems a powerful effort at establishing a new standard of poetical diction, of the rhetoric of poetry; but to waive every other objection it is essentially archaic, biblical a good deal, and so on: now that is a thing that can never last; a perfect style must be of its age.' Before that, he had written to Bridges: 'Swinburne's genius is astonishing, but it will, I think, only do one thing.' By 1885, Swinburne's attempt to describe a sunset—perhaps in *Evening on the Broads* (*Studies in Song*, 1880)—calls forth much more explicit criticism:

> Either in fact he does not see nature at all or else he overlays the landscape with such phantasmata, secondary images, and what not of a delirium-tremendous imagination that the result is a kind of bloody broth: you know what I mean. At any rate there is no picture.

Hopkins was still preoccupied with Swinburne in the last letters he wrote to both Dixon and Bridges. For *Locrine's* 'music of words' and 'distinctive poetic diction, a style properly so called', he had high praise; but his reservation is more important: 'The diction is Elizabethan or nearly: not one sentence is properly modern.' Most important of all is his criticism, in his final letter to Bridges, of Swinburne's *Poems and Ballads* : 'He has no real understanding of rhythm, and though he sometimes hits brilliantly at other times he misses badly.'

These are the faults—archaic diction and insufficiently wrought rhythm—that finally damn Swinburne for Hopkins (as, indeed, they have damned Swinburne for perhaps most twentieth-century readers). And Hopkins's perception of them points unerringly to the two qualities that, above all, made Hopkins himself, as a Victorian, a unique poetic innovator: a determination to use the resources of *current* idiom to the utmost, to break down the conventional barriers between the spoken language of the day and 'the language of poetry'; and an equal determination to forge a new rhythm that would be functional to the sense of the poem, that would, as he put it, 'fetch out' its meaning.

In his best known comment on poetic language, Hopkins wrote to Bridges on 14 August 1879:

> It seems to me that the poetical language of an age shd. be the current language heightened, to any degree heightened and unlike itself, but not (I mean normally: passing freaks and graces are another thing) an obsolete one. This is Shakespeare's and Milton's practice and the want of it will be fatal to Tennyson's Idylls and plays, to Swinburne, and perhaps to Morris.

The reference to Shakespeare is all-important. Hopkins's use of language *is* Shakespearean: he makes words work, dramatically and physically, in a way quite outside the capacity—or indeed, one suspects, the desire—of any of his poetic contemporaries. Moreover, the reference to both Shakespeare and Milton insists on the fact (denied by such critics as Yvor Winters and Donald Davie) that Hopkins saw himself as *within* the great English poetic tradition: as an innovator but, through his innovations, a restorer.

The second part of Hopkins's comment to Bridges safeguards, in fact, a great deal of what the poet can do to the current language, without its becoming 'obsolete'. It safeguards, as he puts it, heightening 'to any degree', 'passing graces', even 'passing freaks'. It justifies in fact almost all the devices that Hopkins adopted to make words *tell*, the devices that we respond to as pure Hopkins but which demand, as with no other of his contemporaries, a concentration of response, not only to experience what he is saying, but often simply to understand it. It is this heightening of language, then, that is continually brought about by Hopkins's alliteration, chiming of consonants, word repetitions, interior rhymes, partial assonance, all that he defended as achieving 'more brilliancy, starriness, quain, margaretting'. Heightening explains too the idiosyncrasies or distortions of syntax—the inversions, telescopings, omission of relative pronouns—which he had to explain in letter after letter to Bridges and Dixon. All contribute to concentrating and energizing the meaning, by lessening or simply omitting what did not matter to him. How much he intended the result to have some of the qualities of drama, albeit a very personal drama, is shown by his commendation, again to Bridges, of what he called 'a nameless quality, which is of the first importance, both in oratory and drama'.

> I sometimes [he says] call it *bidding*: I mean the art or virtue of saying everything right *to* or *at* the hearer, interesting him, holding him in his attitude of correspondent or addressed or at least concerned, making it everywhere an act of intercourse—and of discarding everything that does not bid, does not tell.

Sprung rhythm

It is quite remarkable that, after seven years poetic silence, Hopkins should write a poem so utterly different in power and kind from the substantially Victorian poems he had written before: a poem that displays, already fully-fledged and with complete assurance, all his technical innovations. We know, from what he wrote to Dixon about the origin of *The Wreck of the Deutschland*, the part his experiments with rhythm played: 'I had long had haunting my ear the echo of a new rhythm which now I realised on paper.' But he had also been thinking a great deal about the structure of poetic language itself; and, above all, about how it can attain the maximum stress or emphasis. In 1873–74, as part of his Jesuit training, Hopkins had taught Rhetoric at Manresa House, Roehampton. Some of his lecture notes survive: one set marked 'Rhythm and the other structural parts of Rhetoric—verse', and a short fragment, marked 'Poetry and verse'. They show how he had already extended his concept of inscape, distinctive form, from natural or concrete objects to poetry itself. 'Poetry', runs his opening note on 'Poetry and verse', 'is in fact speech only employed to carry the inscape of speech for the inscape's sake'; and then—making clearer his own shorthand —it is 'speech framed to be heard for its own sake and interest even over and above its interest or meaning'. The *shape* and *sound* of a poem matter, then, intensely.

The shape of poetry had long interested Hopkins. In an undergraduate essay, 'Poetic Diction', he had explored one of its traditional forms. 'The structure of poetry', he wrote, 'is that of continuous parallelism, ranging from the technical so-called Parallelisms of

Hebrew poetry and the antiphons of Church music up to the intricacy of Greek or Italian or English verse.' His notes on Rhetoric show that sound now interested him even more. In 'Poetic Diction' he had seen poetry as calling for 'an emphasis of structure stronger than the common construction of sentences gives'. He now breaks this down further and demands 'stress or emphasis, and pitch or intonation, of single syllables one against another'; then a *continuous* stress 'running through the sentence and setting word against word as stronger or as higher pitched'. The relevance of all this to his own poetic practice is obvious.

Throughout these notes, Hopkins's terms are of speech—or music —*heard*. As he told Bridges again and again, he wanted his own poems to be read aloud:

> My verse is less to be read than heard . . . it is oratorical, that is, the rhythm is so.

> To do the Eurydice any kind of justice you must not slovenly read it with the eyes but with your ears, as if the paper were declaiming it at you. For instance, the line 'she had come from a cruise training seamen', read without stress and declaim, is mere Lloyd's Shipping Intelligence; properly read it is quite a different thing. Stress is the life of it.
>
> Take breath and read it with the ears, as I always wish to be read, and my verse becomes all right.

This insistence on performance, as the true and traditional medium of any art, is the subject of an important letter Hopkins wrote to his youngest brother Everard, published by Fr Anthony Bischoff in 1972. It was written in Ireland in November 1885:

> I am sweetly soothed by your saying that you cd. make any one understand my poem by reciting it well. That is what I always hoped, thought, and said: it is my precise aim. . . . Every art . . . and every work of art has its own play or performance. The play or performance of a stage-play is the playing it on the boards, the stage: reading it, much more writing it, is not its performance. The performance of a symphony is not the scoring it however elaborately; it is in the concert room, by the orchestra, and then and there only. A picture is performed, or performs, when anyone looks at it in the proper and intended light. A house performs when it is now built and lived in. To come nearer: books play, perform, or are played and performed when they are read. . . . Poetry was originally meant for either singing or reciting.

But then, he goes on, it was recorded, to be read 'by one reader, alone, to himself, with the eyes only'. 'This is not the true nature of poetry, the darling child of speech, of lips and spoken utterance:

it must be spoken; *till it is spoken it is not performed*, it does not perform, it is not itself.'

The letter continues with a defence of what he called sprung rhythm, the new rhythm he told Dixon in October 1878 had long been 'haunting' his ear. His own explanation of it in the Preface he wrote for the MS book of his poems in *c.* 1883 is straightforward enough, but the technical elaborations he added to it have caused difficulty. He explained it to Dixon much more simply: 'To speak shortly, it consists in scanning by accents or stresses alone, without any account of the number of syllables, so that a foot may be one long syllable or it may be many light and one strong.' In a further letter he was simpler still: 'This then is the essence of sprung rhythm: *One stress makes one foot*, no matter how many or few the syllables.' There were two further points about it he was intent on making clear: that he had not invented it—like his use of current language, it was part of the English tradition; and that it was nearest to the rhythms of speech and prose.

Once again, in not using a regular metre scanned by syllables or standard running rhythm, Hopkins was making a bold innovation that shocked a prosodist like Bridges; but he was determined to show that he had tradition behind him. Thus he continued to Dixon: 'I do not say the idea is altogether new; there are hints of it in music, in nursery rhymes and popular jingles, in the poets themselves.' A main source, as he said in the same letter, he had found in the 'irregular' choruses of Milton's *Samson Agonistes*. The nearness of sprung rhythm to the rhythms of speech shows again Hopkins's genius for finding the way to the maximum sound-impact of words in poetry. It also gave him the sense of freedom that is an integral —perhaps, ultimately, the most exciting—element in his poems. 'Why do I employ sprung rhythm at all?' he wrote to Bridges. 'Because it is the nearest to the rhythm of prose, that is the native and natural rhythm of speech, the least forced, the most rhetorical and emphatic of all possible rhythms.' It gave him infinitely greater flexibility than syllabic metre. Sprung rhythm itself brings about the essential qualities he wanted his poetry to possess, as he told his brother Everard in the letter already quoted: 'Sprung rhythm gives back to poetry its true soul and self. As poetry is emphatically speech, speech purged of dross like gold in the furnace, so it must have emphatically the essential elements of speech. Now emphasis itself, stress, is one of these: sprung rhythm makes verse stressy.'

The sense of freedom and energy generated by Hopkins's poetry has led some critics to believe that his 'new rhythm' was really intuitive; and that he developed his theory of sprung rhythm to justify his practice, rather than the reverse. This can obviously not be proved or disproved: all we can say is that he put the case for the effectiveness of sprung rhythm with passionate cogency; and that his poems themselves magnificently vindicate its use. Another view put forward (by Harold Whitehall in 'Hopkins's sprung rhythm', *The Kenyon Critics*, 1937) is that Hopkins's innovations in rhythm were what really mattered to him, were the ultimate outlet for his poetic energy; and that his verbal devices were there to serve them. On this view, a great deal of Hopkins's distinctive style—the alliteration, chiming of consonants, repetition of word and syllable— is used to reinforce or 'overstress' the strong stresses in the rhythm. It is true that in almost any mature Hopkins poem we quickly, if subconsciously, learn to anticipate certain sounds or sound combinations, so that, each time they are repeated, we give them slightly more emphasis than usual. The more complex the stress pattern, the more frequent the devices. The examples that Whitehall gives in his essay certainly support this functional 'overstressing'.

What is certain is that orthodox Victorian critics would not tolerate Hopkins's experiments in either language or rhythm. Patmore was quite justified when, writing to Hopkins is 1884 about 'the *Gallery* Gods—i.e. the common run of "Nineteenth Century", "Fortnightly" & such critics', he said: 'I feel *absolutely* sure that you would never conciliate *them*.' Hopkins had been unable to 'conciliate' the Jesuit editor of *The Month*, Fr Henry Coleridge, with either *The Wreck of the Deutschland* or *The Loss of the Eurydice*, neither of which, as Hopkins put it, they 'dared publish'. He made only one other attempt to publish when, in 1881, on Canon Dixon's encouragement, he sent three sonnets for a selection being edited by Hall Caine. This too came to grief because, as Hall Caine wrote to him, the purpose of his anthology was to 'demonstrate the impossibility of improving upon the acknowledged structure whether as to rhyme-scheme or measure'. 'Poor soul', Hopkins wrote to Bridges, 'he writes to me as to a she bear robbed of her cubs.'

Bridges's own position was an ambivalent one. He rushed to his friend's defence by writing an angry letter to Hall Caine and himself refusing to contribute to the anthology. Whatever his strictures to Hopkins himself, he told Dixon that Hopkins's poems 'more carried him out of himself than those of any one'; and, as Patmore later told Hopkins, he 'spoke with the sincerest admiration and *love* of your poetry'. But friendship and genuine appreciation could not stifle the orthodox Victorian in Bridges. When, after Hopkins's death, he selected eleven of his poems (including extracts) for A.H. Miles's *Poets and Poetry of the Century* [1893], and six poems (two of them extracts) for his own anthology, *The Spirit of Man*, 1915, he chose the easier and less experimental ones. And in the *Preface to Notes* to his edition of Hopkins's *Poems*, 1918, after enumerating the 'faults of style' under the headings 'Oddity', 'Obscurity', 'Omission of Relative Pronoun', 'Identical Forms', 'Homophones', and 'Rhymes', he pointed clearly to the central Victorian canon of taste that had until then condemned Hopkins: 'These blemishes in the poet's style are of such quality and magnitude as to deny him a hearing from those who love a continuous literary decorum and are grown to be intolerant of its absence.'

Anglo-Saxon and Welsh poetry

It is impossible to read Hopkins without being aware of his strong preference for words of native, Old English origin, over often more common Latinate words. Many are monosyllables; many more compounds: together they give much of both the power and the rootedness (what he called the 'keepings') of his poetry. The monosyllables are often verbs:

> Generations have trod, have trod, have trod;
> And all is seared with trade; bleared, smeared with toil;
> And wears man's smudge and shares man's smell: the soil
> Is bare now, nor can foot feel, being shod.

> *(God's Grandeur)*

The compounds are often invented: 'silk-sack', 'wilful-wavier', 'Meal-drift' *(Hurrahing in Harvest)*; 'dare-gale', 'bone-house', 'song-fowl' *(The Caged Skylark)*. The lists of words, to show connection or etymology, that he made in his undergraduate diaries, show the same preference: 'Grind, gride, girt, grit, groat . . . '; 'Shear, shred, potsherd, shard.'

When he was writing his lecture notes on Rhetoric, in 1873–74, his main interest had moved to rhythm and alliteration. Although he had not yet studied Anglo-Saxon nor read *Piers Plowman*, he knew that the stress rhythm he was to experiment with was the staple of Old English alliterative verse. One of the examples he gives in his notes, to show 'rhythm without count of syllable', was from *Piers Plowman*, the opening lines of *The Vision of Holy Church*:

> What this moúntain beméneth/and this dérke dále,
> And this féld, fúl of fólk/I scháll yow feíre schéwe.

It was not until 1882 that he both read *Piers Plowman* and studied Anglo-Saxon. The poem as such he did not think much of; but he was able now to show that, in using sprung rhythm, he was following a tradition that went back to Old English verse. 'So far as I know', he wrote to Bridges that October, defending sprung rhythm, 'it existed in full force in Anglo Saxon verse and in great beauty; in a degraded and doggrel shape in *Piers Ploughman* (I am reading that famous poem and am coming to the conclusion that it is not worth reading).' A month later Hopkins told him that he was 'learning Anglosaxon and it is a vastly superior thing to what we have now'. But it was now the language that excited him. He had just read the

Dorset dialect poet William Barnes's *An Outline of English Speech-craft*, written in 'a sort of modern Anglosaxon'. Hopkins was sympathetic, but knew that to try to put the clock back was hopeless:

> It makes one weep to think what English might have been; for in spite of all that Shakespere and Milton have done with the compound I cannot doubt that no beauty in a language can make up for want of purity. . . . He calls degrees of comparison pitches of suchness: we *ought* to call them so, but alas!

For the influence of Welsh poetry on Hopkins there is much more evidence.

'I have always looked on myself as half Welsh and so I warm to them', Hopkins wrote to his mother soon after arriving at St Beuno's, in North Wales, in September 1874. 'Always to me a mother of Muses' was his description of Wales in 1886, after a short holiday there. He was of course thinking by then of the three years he had spent at St Beuno's, in which he had written *The Wreck of the Deutschland* and his happiest sonnets. And both the Welsh landscape and its mythology—particularly the legend of St Beuno and St Winifred—continued to have for him the 'instress and charm' he had felt on his first arrival. He had then learnt Welsh, taught by a Miss Susannah Jones; and though he told Baillie in January 1877 that he found 'the greatest difficulty . . . in understanding it when spoken' and could 'make little way with' the poetry, he was being over-modest. For the previous April he had written a *cywydd* (a Welsh seven-syllable-lined poem) to celebrate the silver jubilee of the first Roman Catholic Bishop of Shrewsbury; and it seems all but certain, on internal evidence, that he also translated into Welsh the Latin hymn, *O Deus, Ego amo te*.

What is quite certain is the debt Hopkins acknowledged to classical Welsh poetry. Among the 'oddnesses' of *The Wreck of the Deutschland*, he told Dixon, were 'certain chimes suggested by the Welsh poetry I had been reading (what they call *cynghanedd*)'; and, enclosing two sonnets 'with rhythmical experiments' (probably *God's Grandeur* and *The Starlight Night*) to Bridges in April 1877, he wrote to him: 'The chiming of consonants I got in part from the Welsh, which is very rich in sound and imagery.' Five years later he implied that this influence was a passing phase. *The Sea and the Skylark* (Rhyl, May 1877) was, he told Bridges, 'written in my Welsh days, in my salad days, when I was fascinated with *cynghanedd* or consonant-chime'.

In an article published in the *Modern Language Review*, July 1943, Gweneth Lilly showed in detail with what skill Hopkins had mastered the device of *cynghanedd*, with its elaborate system of alliteration combined with internal rhyme; or, rather, the different kinds of *cynghanedd*, with their different patterns of alliteration and rhyme. She also showed, perhaps more importantly, how fruitfully classical

Welsh poetry, with its traditional respect for form and music, chimed in with Hopkins's own poetic aims of emphasis and stress. There are parallels beyond the 'chiming' consonants that Hopkins explicitly acknowledged: the omission of pronouns and relatives, the wide use of compounds, inversions of word order, exclamations that interrupt sentences. All these help to give the concentration that is integral to both classical Welsh poetry and to Hopkins. Above all, Hopkins never uses the *cynghanedd* simply as decoration. Like the sprung rhythm in which Welsh poetry, as he pointed out, was also written, he uses it organically to 'fetch out' his meaning. If we take the line from stanza 7 of *The Wreck of the Deutschland*, 'Warm-laid grave of a womb-life grey', as a perfect example of the *cynghanedd*, we also realize how strongly the alliteration and consonantal chiming emphasize the paradox of its subject, Christ's incarnation. So, as Gweneth Lilly points out, it happens throughout Hopkins's poetry. Technically, the Welsh influence was hardly a passing phase: chiming of consonants goes on to the end. But, as a truly original poet, Hopkins uses this, like so many other devices, for his own poetic ends and in his own unique way: so that the question of continuing influence seems no longer relevant.

Three friends and literary correspondents: Robert Bridges, R.W. Dixon, and Coventry Patmore

Averse as he was to publication of his poems, after the Jesuit magazine, the *Month*, had refused both *The Wreck of the Deutschland* and *The Loss of the Eurydice*, Hopkins knew that, to continue writing poetry at all, he had to have an audience. 'I must absolutely have encouragement as much as crops rain', he confessed to Bridges in 1885. Much earlier, after Bridges had harshly criticized *The Wreck of the Deutschland*, he had written to him: 'I do not write for the public. You are my public and I hope to convert you.' Three poets in fact constituted Hopkins's public: Robert Bridges, R.W. Dixon and Coventry Patmore. They were the only systematic readers of his poems in his lifetime. Hopkins's letters to Bridges and his letters to and from Dixon and Patmore have all been edited (by C.C. Abbott): they fill two and a half substantial volumes. The major gap is Bridges's letters to Hopkins, which Bridges himself destroyed after his friend's death. All three correspondences bear striking testimony to the importance that Hopkins gave to poetry—that of his three friends, as well as his own —during the twelve years that he was a busy Jesuit priest; they show his remarkable powers of meticulous criticism of poetry utterly different from his own; and they show the respect with which it was treated. But the three friendships the letters record were very different.

When Hopkins first wrote to Dixon from Stonyhurst in June 1878

—a totally unexpected letter of praise for his poems—he was thirty-three and Dixon twelve years older. Sympathy for each other's character soon followed admiration for each other's poems; and the friendship that developed lasted for life. But it was kept going entirely by letter; they met only once. Hopkins did not meet Patmore until 1883; and only for a few days after that. Patmore, a fellow-Catholic, was then sixty-one and had virtually given up writing poetry. But he quickly realized Hopkins's skill and sensitivity as a critic and asked him for his help in preparing a new edition of the four volumes he had already published. He read Hopkins's own poems, but confessed he did not understand most of them. So the letters are mostly confined to a minute discussion of Patmore's work. Both these friendships, then, were essentially literary; and that with Patmore remained very formal (in their salutations they only progressed from 'My Dear Sir' to 'My Dear Mr—'). The friendship with Bridges was totally different. It was literary, in that the central interest of their letters was increasingly each other's poems, besides poetry itself, prosody, rhythm, poetic experiments. But it was also intimate; and this, despite Bridges's self-confessed 'unconquerable repugnance to the full-blown Roman theology'. Hopkins and Bridges were the same age; they met as Oxford undergraduates and by the end of their second year, in 1865, were already close friends. After 1868 when Hopkins entered the Jesuit novitiate, their friendship was sustained (with interruptions) mainly by letter. Jean-Georges Ritz, in his sympathetic study of the two men, has calculated that thereafter they met only about twelve times. But their shared Oxford memories were clearly of the utmost importance to both of them; and the friendship, for Hopkins, was crucial. Bridges has the natural right of first place in any discussion of Hopkins's personal life.

ROBERT BRIDGES For all Bridges's acclaim as a poet in the early decades of this century, he remains a somewhat elusive figure. This was his own wish. He made it clear that he wanted no biography written. He destroyed his letters to R.W. Dixon as well as to Hopkins; and indeed to many other friends as well. He had a natural restraint that went with his deep and lifelong love of the Classics. Epithets used by the friends of his final years include 'bearish' and even 'grumpy'; they also testify to his great personal charm and warmth of friendship, besides his magnificent looks. He certainly had a great gift for friendship; and much of what we do know of his more personal life comes from the memoirs he wrote of three friends, D.M. Dolben, R.W. Dixon and the philologist Henry Bradley. He planned to write a memoir of Hopkins, to precede a selection of his poems, in 1889, a few months after his friend's death. But the memoir was never written and his edition of Hopkins's poems—the 'lov'd legacy' he

Robert Bridges, c. *1863*

had preserved for so long—he delayed until 1918. Both the delay and his 'Preface to Notes', which, although praising 'exquisite beauties', contained harsh criticisms of Hopkins's innovations, have antagonised lovers of Hopkins ever since.

The photographs of Hopkins and Bridges as undergraduates, (frontispiece and page 76), accentuate their differences of temperament. Bridges is clearly much the more robust and masculine. Hopkins was in no conventional sense a 'leader' nor an athlete. Many have found the friendship difficult to account for. Herbert Read, in an early essay on Hopkins (1936), assumed that for Hopkins the attraction was 'instinctive, even physical'; and this must be at any rate partly true. Several of Hopkins's poems show his susceptibility to masculine beauty; and in one letter to Bridges he shows his physical admiration for him with his usual outspoken candour: 'I think then no one can admire beauty of the body more than I do, and it is of course a comfort to find beauty in a friend or a friend in beauty' (22 October 1879). But they had, in fact, many shared interests from the beginning. Both came up to Oxford strongly High Church, Bridges intending to take Orders—as his family imagined Hopkins would; both were intensely interested in music, in the Classics (Bridges, like Hopkins, read Greats), in language and in prosody. Hopkins knew that his friend composed Airs long before he discovered that he was a poet.

There are only two references to Bridges in Hopkins's undergraduate Diaries, both—rather revealingly—among his notes for confession made during 1865: 'Nothing read, not very culpable perhaps, but chiefly through going to Bridges in the evening'; and 'Foolish gossipy way with Bridges.' Hopkins's scruples, as such notes show, began long before he became a Catholic. Hopkins's belief in Bridges as the friend he could trust above all dates from the following year, 1866, when he spent the first three weeks of September staying with him and his family in Rochdale, Lancashire. Hopkins was in a critical state of mind, midway between his conversion (that July) and his reception by Newman on his way home from Rochdale; and, without knowing its cause till Hopkins was on the point of leaving, Bridges clearly showed great sympathy. 'I can never thank you enough for yr. kindness at that time', Hopkins wrote to him; and, in the same letter: 'Notwithstanding my anxiety . . . it gives me more delight to think of the time at Rochdale than any other time whatever that I can remember.' In explaining to Bridges, who was hurt, why he could not tell him of his conversion, Hopkins was scrupulous, firm, but gentle. They are the qualities that did much to cement a friendship that (as many Victorian friendships did) could easily have foundered on strongly felt religious differences. Moreover, Hopkins could laugh at himself (we have less evidence that Bridges could), as his letters often show.

For the next year, that began with Hopkins teaching for Newman at the Oratory School, Birmingham, and Bridges at Oxford preparing for Greats, Hopkins's letters are relaxed, factual, but affectionate (his first one addressed 'Dearest Bridges' was in November 1867; the only letter of his own that Bridges kept, his last, written during Hopkins's final illness, begins 'Dearest Gerard'). There are more attempts at meetings than meetings themselves. Then in June 1868 Hopkins announced that he was to enter the Jesuit novitiate at Roehampton that autumn. We do not have Bridges's reaction; but we know his profound dislike of the Jesuits. Moreover, after travel abroad, Bridges soon began his own career as a doctor. He visited Hopkins at Roehampton in October 1869 and there was apparently an estrangement, for which Hopkins took the blame. That was in his next letter a year and a half later; and it was followed in August 1871 by what Hopkins later called his 'red letter', defending ideal Communism: 'Horrible to say, in a manner I am a Communist. Their ideal bating some things is nobler than that professed by any secular statesman I know of (I must own I live in bat-light and shoot at a venture). Besides it is just.' Bridges, a deep-dyed Conservative, was clearly shocked by this letter and never answered it. There was no communication between them for two and a half years. It was Hopkins who began the correspondence again, in January 1874, on discovering, from an *Academy* review of Bridges's *Poems*, 1873, that his friend wrote poetry.

Hopkins's move in September 1874 to North Wales, to study theology for three years, made meetings few and far between; and letters were still sparse. But in February or March 1877 Bridges sent Hopkins his last two collections of poems, *The Growth of Love* and *Carmen Elegiacum*; and in April Hopkins sent back his first detailed criticism. This first long letter devoted to the practice of poetry sets the tone of many of the more than 140 letters or cards Hopkins wrote to Bridges before his death, twelve years later. Hopkins is generous, candid, authoritatively exact in both praise and blame, totally concerned; he is also more personal and relaxed than with anyone else he wrote to, and at times he can enjoy his sharp sense of humour. The praise makes the occasional rebuke disarmingly just:

> The sonnets are truly beautiful, breathing a grave and feeling genius, and make me proud of you (which by the by is not the same as for you to be proud of yourself: I say it because you always were and I see you still are given to conceit ...)

And, two and a half years later:

> You seem to want to be told over again that you have genius and are a poet and your verses beautiful. ... You want perhaps to be told more in particular. I am not the best to tell you, being biassed

by love, and yet I am too. ... If I were not your friend I shd. wish to be the friend of the man who wrote your poems. They shew the eye for pure beauty and they shew, my dearest, besides, the character which is much more rare and precious.

The frank avowal of affection was clearly vital to Hopkins. But it must have been severely strained by the reception Bridges gave to the poems that Hopkins now sent him.

For Hopkins's long letter of April 1877, criticizing Bridges's poems, chimed in with his own return to writing poetry. He enclosed two sonnets with that letter (probably *God's Grandeur* and *The Starlight Night*) with the warning, 'And don't *you* say *my* lines don't scan'; and in August he sent him *The Wreck of the Deutschland*. Bridges's description of the poem in his edition of Hopkins's poems is now notorious: it 'stands ... in the front of his book, like a great dragon folded in the gate to forbid all entrance'. To Hopkins himself he described it as 'presumptious [*thus*] jugglery'—and sent him a parody, to show he understood the metre. Bridges was not alone in his incomprehension and dislike of Hopkins's experiments in *The Wreck of the Deutschland*: *The Month* declined to publish it; and Coventry Patmore, for all his respect for Hopkins, could never, he said, reconcile himself to its 'strangeness'. But Hopkins was considerably hurt by Bridges's reaction. 'I cannot think of altering anything', he replied. 'Why shd. I? I do not write for the public. You are my public and I hope to convert you./You say you wd. not for any money read my poem again. Nevertheless I beg you will. Besides money, you know, there is love.' The following May Hopkins sent him *The Loss of the Eurydice*; but Bridges's refusal to re-read *The Wreck of the Deutschland* still clearly rankled, and it drew from Hopkins one of his most ingenious and obviously enjoyed critical analogues:

Write no bilgewater about it [*The Eurydice*]: I will presently tell you what that is and till then excuse the term. ... Now they say that vessels sailing from the port of London will take (perhaps it should be/used once to take) Thames water for the voyage: it was foul and stunk at first as the ship worked but by degrees casting its filth was in a few days very pure and sweet and wholesome and better than any water in the world. However that maybe [*thus*], it is true to my purpose. When a new thing, such as my ventures in the Deutschland are, is presented us our first criticisms are not our truest, best, most homefelt, or most lasting but what come easiest on the instant. They are barbarous and like what the ignorant and the ruck say. This was so with you. The Deutschland on her first run worked very much and unsettled you, thickening and clouding your mind with vulgar mudbottom and common sewage (I see that I am going it with the image) and just then unhappily you *drew off* your criticisms all stinking (a necessity now

79

of the image) and bilgy, whereas if you had let your thoughts cast themselves they would have been clearer in themselves and more to my taste too. I did not heed them therefore, perceiving they were a first drawing-off. Same of the Eurydice—which being short and easy please read more than once.

The Loss of the Eurydice Bridges did praise. But from now on two things are clear in Hopkins's letters: his sharp sensitivity to criticism and his confidence in his technical experiments. 'As for affectation,' he now wrote—with absolute justification—'I do not believe I am guilty of it: you should point out instances, but as long as mere novelty and boldness strikes you as affectation your criticism strikes me as—as water of the Lower Isis.' This confidence in his poetic technique never left him. One of the most valuable results of his friendship with Bridges was that he felt compelled, again and again, to explain to him what he was doing, the effects he was aiming at; indeed, many times he had to send him line-by-line explanations of whole poems. Hopkins was totally articulate about his own aims: so his letters to Bridges contain one of the most revealing defences we possess of any poet's practice and poetic beliefs. Sharply sensitive as he was, he clearly took some note of Bridges's objections to his 'obscurities' and 'eccentricities'. Inviting 'minute criticism' of his sonnet *Andromeda*, he wrote to him: 'I endeavoured in it at a more Miltonic plainness and severity than I have anywhere else'; and of his late sonnet *St Alphonsus Rodriguez*, 'The sonnet (I say it snorting) aims at being intelligible.' At the same time he showed a remarkable sympathy for a style quite unlike his own in his meticulous criticism of Bridges's poems. In poem after poem he suggested amendments to give more force or more exactness or greater metrical subtlety; and later editions of Bridges's poems show how many of them Bridges adopted. An immense amount of Hopkins's imaginative vitality went into this criticism; there was clearly an element in it of compensation, when he felt his own creative impulses drying up.

But Hopkins's letters to Bridges are also a storehouse of all their shared interests: in music, prosody, language, Milton, the contemporary poetic scene. From 1881 on, indeed, Hopkins's own musical compositions become a main subject of letters. In April of that year he wrote to Bridges:

> Every impulse and spring of art seems to have died in me, except for music, and that I pursue under almost an impossibility of getting on. Nevertheless, I still put down my pieces, for the airs seem worth it; they seem to me to have something in them which other modern music has not got.

Composing undoubtedly helped him greatly during his depressed last years in Dublin; and, in his letters to Bridges from Ireland, right up to the final one, there is more about his music than his poems. John Stevens, in his Appendix on Hopkins as Musician, in *The Journals and Papers*, stresses that his musical gift, whatever it might have become, was 'a gift for *melody*'. He gives evidence for settings by Hopkins to twenty-seven songs and poems, including four of his own, five by Bridges and four by Dixon, the music to about half of which has survived. This John Stevens gives.

Above all, Bridges was Hopkins's confidant, when he desperately needed one in his five years of growing desolation in Dublin. Other friends, Dixon and Baillie, heard something of his melancholy, but it was to Bridges that he fully unburdened himself.

It is essentially a sense of trust that Hopkins's letters to Bridges show: a trust sufficient to override Bridges's antipathy to his religion and incomprehension of much of his poetry. He was still, as Hopkins told him, his 'public'; and Hopkins still hoped—at any rate poetically—to 'convert' him. This makes Bridges's delay of thirty years in publishing his poems and his failure to write a memoir of him the more surprising. Without understanding it, he recognized Hopkins's genius; he had scrupulously kept all Hopkins's poems in either manuscript or copy; he certainly intended to publish them. A plan to include some in a proposed privately printed anthology in 1880, during Hopkins's lifetime, came to nothing. A further plan, for both poems and memoir, a few months after Hopkins's death, went much further but was eventually dropped. Instead, Bridges released a few of Hopkins's poems to anthologies over the next twenty-five years, culminating in six poems and parts of poems in his own *The Spirit of Man*, 1915. It was the interest aroused in Hopkins's poems in *The Spirit of Man* that led to Bridges's complete edition of 1918. The letters that he wrote to Kate Hopkins, Gerard's sister (his mother, still alive, was ninety-six), show the care that he devoted to it. The fact that that edition of 750 copies took twelve years to sell out shows that Bridges's earlier apprehensions about the reception of his friend's innovations were not ill-founded. Relatively few people were ready for them until the 1930s.

R.W. DIXON   Dixon and Hopkins, despite the difference in their ages and vocations, were in many ways remarkably kindred spirits. For each, Oxford was a crucial experience: for Dixon, not the University as such, nor his College (Pembroke), both of which—unlike Hopkins a decade later—he found dispiritingly uninspired and unintellectual; but the group of friends he made there and valued for life. Each, for a time, found his ideals embodied in the values of the Middle Ages; though, for Dixon, this habit of mind lasted much longer and indeed marked most of his poetry. Each valued the visual world immensely and had thoughts of becoming a painter. And perhaps most importantly for the friendship they developed, each was exceptionally finely tempered in mind, sensitive and scrupulous; their understanding and appreciation of each other's poems was based on a deep, if rarely stated, sympathy for each other's spiritual conflicts (for Dixon, these were more apparent several years after Hopkins's death).

When Dixon received Hopkins's first letter in early June 1878, he was at a very low ebb: his wife had died two years before; he was suffering from chronic ill-health; he felt isolated in his country vicarage; his poems had been virtually ignored. And now, out of the blue, came Hopkins's deeply-felt admiration: 'I became so fond of [*Christ's Company*] that I made it ... a part of my own mind'; individual poems were full of 'tenderness', 'richness of colouring', 'the pathos of nature and landscape'. The impact such a letter made is hardly surprising: he was, Dixon replied, 'shaken to the very centre'. From then until less than a year before his death Hopkins gave Dixon—as he gave Bridges—both appreciation and minute criticism: it was, he told Dixon, 'a labour of love', 'one of the best pleasures of life'. But the encouragement was mutual. Within a year Dixon had asked to see Hopkins's own poems; and his recognition of Hopkins's genius was immediate: 'I have your Poems and have read them I cannot say with what delight, astonishment, & admiration. They are among the most extraordinary I ever read & amazingly original.' From then on he joined Bridges as Hopkins's 'audience'. He may not have understood Hopkins's innovations more than Bridges did, but he was infinitely more humble in accepting that as his own failure; and in one phrase (since become famous), taken from *Ezekiel*, he went to the heart of the quality in Hopkins's poems that so affected him: they had, he wrote, in October 1881, 'a right temper which goes to the point of the terrible; the terrible crystal'. But if he did not understand Hopkins's experiments, he understood —and indeed later suffered from himself—the scruples about writing poetry that could torment the priest. Hopkins's confession that he had destroyed his poems when he became a Jesuit, 'and meant to write no more', caused Dixon genuine anguish. Imploring him to continue, Dixon wrote: 'Surely one vocation cannot destroy another: and such a Society as yours will not remain ignorant that you have such gifts as have seldom been given by God to man.'

But if he could persuade Hopkins to continue writing, Dixon could not break down his determined resistance to publication. He wished to mention Hopkins, as a Jesuit poet, in a footnote to his *History of the Church of England*; he then proposed sending the *The Loss of the Eurydice* to a Carlisle newspaper. Both suggestions were refused, the second with almost horrified dismay. Dixon himself, as he often told Hopkins, gained immeasurably from his minute criticism. In addition, Hopkins introduced him, by letter, to Bridges; and the two became firm friends and admirers of each other's work. Dixon's own spirits revived: he returned to writing poetry and completed his epic,

Richard Watson Dixon

Mano, his most substantial poem. For almost a decade these three 'hidden poets' became—if mainly through letters—in James Sambrook's phrase, taken from Dixon's group of Oxford friends' name for themselves, a 'second Brotherhood'.

Hopkins and Dixon met once only, for a few hours, between trains at Carlisle. It was not a great success: Hopkins found Dixon shy and, for himself, could not communicate his own feelings. But Bridges visited Dixon many times at his final living in Warkworth, Northumberland. It is Bridges who has left the most affectionate portrait of him at the end of his *Memoir*:

This great ingenuous being went about among men almost un-recognized, though influencing nearly every one with whom he came in contact. As he respected every man, he won respect from all, and any lengthened intercourse with him awoke the best affinities of his associates who became infected with his grace.

Hopkins, in a letter to Bridges on the ultimate superiority of 'the gentleman' to the artist, used Dixon to illustrate his point: 'And this adds a charm to everything Canon Dixon writes, that you feel he is a gentleman and thinks like one.' It was the highest praise he could give.

COVENTRY PATMORE   When Coventry Patmore was entrusted to Hopkins's care for the Stonyhurst Speech Day, in late July 1883, he had already made, and to some extent lost, a reputation as a poet. He was now a striking and patrician-looking man of sixty-one; a strong Tory; a Catholic convert; and financially independent. Hopkins had long known his poetry, and greatly admired it. He had some reservations, he told Bridges in May 1879; 'but for insight he beats all our living poets, his insight is really profound, and he has an exquisiteness, farfetchedness, of imagery worthy of the best things of the Caroline age'. The two men clearly took strongly to each other. Hopkins introduced him to the poetry of Bridges and Dixon; and Patmore asked Hopkins if he would give him detailed criticisms of his four published volumes of poems for a revised edition: likely to be the last, as he said, in his lifetime. 'I do not know,' wrote Hopkins to Bridges, clearly flattered and delighted, 'but it was bragging to mention this; however now there it is, all blubbering in wet ink.' So, once again, we have Hopkins the meticulous critic, more formal and systematic in the fault-finding he had been asked to carry out than with Bridges or Dixon; but, as with them, acutely sensitive to every nuance of word or rhyme or metre. What is im-pressive is the readiness with which Patmore accepted Hopkins's criticisms. Far from humble by temperament, he was full of gratitude. 'Your careful and subtle fault-finding', he wrote that October, 'is the greatest praise my poetry has ever received.' When the collected edition finally came out in 1886, he wrote to Hopkins: 'My new edn owes very much to you. "It is the last rub that polishes the mirror" (a proverb by the way of my own making & of which I am very proud) and your suggestions have enabled me to give my poems that final rub.'

But, if Patmore found Hopkins invaluable as a critic, Hopkins as a poet was too difficult for him. A few of his simpler poems—'expressed without any obscuring novelty of mode'—he found 'exquisite'; but *The Wreck of the Deutschland* was beyond him.

Coventry Patmore

'System and learned theory', he wrote to Hopkins, 'are manifest in all these experiments; but they seem to me to be *too* manifest. To me they often darken the thought and feeling which all arts and artifices of language should only illustrate; and I often find it as hard to follow you as I have found it to follow the darkest parts of Browning' (a comparison that can hardly have pleased Hopkins).

To Bridges (whose own appreciation of Hopkins puzzled him) Patmore summed up his view of Hopkins's poetry in a phrase that has become famous (or notorious): 'To me his poetry has the effect of pure gold imbedded in masses of unpracticable quartz.' But, he went on, 'his genius is, however, unmistakable, and is lovely and unique in its effects whenever he approximates to the ordinary rules of composition'. And a second letter showed his real and sensitive regard for Hopkins as a man: 'I wish I had not had to tell Hopkins of my objections. But I had either to be silent or to say the truth. . . . I have seldom felt so much attracted towards any man as I have been towards him, and I shall be more sorry than I can say if my criticisms have hurt him.'

In August 1885 Hopkins stayed a few days with the Patmores in Hastings, and there read, at Patmore's request, the MS of a prose work Patmore had been engaged on for many years. Entitled *Sponsa Dei*, it was—as described by Edmund Gosse, who also read it—'an interpretation of the love between the soul and God by an analogy of the love between a woman and a man' (the same theme as parts of *The Unknown Eros*). Patmore had intended it to be published after his death. No one knows what Hopkins said to him after reading it, but he was clearly apprehensive about its publication as it stood. On returning to Dublin, he wrote to Patmore supporting his view that 'anything however high and innocent' *could* suggest something 'low and loathsome', by giving him historical examples of 'the abuses high contemplation is liable to'. It is a stern, even formidable letter. On Christmas Day 1887, after 'much-meditating' on the effect of the MS on Hopkins, Patmore burnt it. To Bridges, after Hopkins's death eighteen months later, Patmore sent an account that was both simplified and dramatized:

> The *authority* of his goodness was so great with me that I threw the manuscript of a little work—a sort of 'Religio Poetae'—into the fire, simply because, when he had read it, he said with a grave look, 'That's telling secrets'. This little book had been the work of ten years' continual meditations, and could not but have made a greater effect than all the rest I have written; but his doubt was final with me.

Dramatized or not, the remarkable impact of Hopkins as a man on the older and established poet remains; it was a tribute to much more than the poet and critic.

Part Two
Critical Survey

Introduction

In his fourteen years as a mature poet, from the end of 1875 to early 1889, Hopkins only wrote, apart from fragments and unfinished poems, forty-nine poems: these are the poems he sent to Robert Bridges, who kept them in a manuscript book, and those found among Hopkins's papers after his death. With a few exceptions (mainly occasional poems), almost all have been greatly admired, though in differing degrees. Choice for inclusion in this survey is bound, therefore, to be to some extent personal. Two factors have particularly influenced it. First, poems have been chosen to show Hopkins's major periods of creativity, however different their causes and the feelings that accompanied them. They include three of the excited sonnets written in North Wales in 1877, and two of the very different, desolate sonnets written in Dublin in 1885. Secondly, several of those included have been widely regarded as 'difficult', in syntax, word coinages, and sometimes imagery; and an attempt has been made to show that the difficulties have often been exaggerated, and that, once they have been solved, the poetic rewards of these poems— perhaps these in particular—are often that much the greater.

The Wreck of the Deutschland

PART THE FIRST

1

Thou mastering me
God! giver of breath and bread;
World's strand, sway of the sea;
Lord of living and dead;
Thou hast bound bones and veins in me, fastened me flesh,
And after it almost unmade, what with dread,
Thy doing: and dost thou touch me afresh?
Over again I feel thy finger and find thee.

2

I did say yes
O at lightning and lashed rod;
Thou heardst me truer than tongue confess
Thy terror, O Christ, O God;
Thou knowest the walls, altar and hour and night:
The swoon of a heart that the sweep and the hurl of thee trod
Hard down with a horror of height:
And the midriff astrain with leaning of, laced with fire of stress.

3

The frown of his face
Before me, the hurtle of hell
Behind, where, where was a, where was a place?
I whirled out wings that spell
And fled with a fling of the heart to the heart of the Host.
My heart, but you were dovewinged, I can tell,
Carrier-witted, I am bold to boast,
To flash from the flame to the flame then, tower from the grace
   to the grace.

4

I am soft sift
In an hourglass—at the wall
Fast, but mined with a motion, a drift,
And it crowds and it combs to the fall;
I steady as a water in a well, to a poise, to a pane,
But roped with, always, all the way down from the tall
Fells or flanks of the voel, a vein
Of the gospel proffer, a pressure, a principle, Christ's gift.

5

I kiss my hand
To the stars, lovely-asunder
Starlight, wafting him out of it; and
Glow, glory in thunder;
Kiss my hand to the dappled-with-damson west:
Since, tho' he is under the world's splendour and wonder,
His mystery must be instressed, stressed;
For I greet him the days I meet him, and bless when I understand.

6

Not out of his bliss
Springs the stress felt
Nor first from heaven (and few know this)
Swings the stroke dealt—
Stroke and a stress that stars and storms deliver,
That guilt is hushed by, hearts are flushed by and melt—
But it rides time like riding a river
(And here the faithful waver, the faithless fable and miss).

7

It dates from day
Of his going in Galilee;
Warm-laid grave of a womb-life grey;
Manger, maiden's knee;
The dense and the driven Passion, and frightful sweat;
Thence the discharge of it, there its swelling to be,
Though felt before, though in high flood yet—
What none would have known of it, only the heart, being hard
at bay,

8

Is out with it! Oh,
We lash with the best or worst
Word last! How a lush-kept plush-capped sloe
Will, mouthed to flesh-burst,
Gush!—flush the man, the being with it, sour or sweet,
Brim, in a flash, full!—Hither then, last or first,
To hero of Calvary, Christ's feet—
Never ask if meaning it, wanting it, warned of it—men go.

9

Be adored among men,
God, three-numberèd form;
Wring thy rebel, dogged in den,
Man's malice, with wrecking and storm.
Beyond saying sweet, past telling of tongue,
Thou art lightning and love, I found it, a winter and warm;
Father and fondler of heart thou hast wrung:
Hast thy dark descending and most art merciful then.

10

With an anvil-ding
And with fire in him forge thy will
Or rather, rather then, stealing as Spring
Through him, melt him but master him still:
Whether at once, as once at a crash Paul,
Or as Austin, a lingering-out swéet skill,
Make mercy in all of us, out of us all
Mastery, but be adored, but be adored King.

PART THE SECOND

11

'Some find me a sword; some
The flange and the rail; flame,
Fang, or flood' goes Death on drum,
And storms bugle his fame.
But wé dream we are rooted in earth—Dust!
Flesh falls within sight of us, we, though our flower the same,
Wave with the meadow, forget that there must
The sour scythe cringe, and the blear share come.

On Saturday sailed from Bremen,
        American-outward-bound,
    Take settler and seamen, tell men with women,
        Two hundred souls in the round—
O Father, not under thy feathers nor ever as guessing
The goal was a shoal, of a fourth the doom to be drowned;
        Yet did the dark side of the bay of thy blessing
Not vault them, the millions of rounds of thy mercy not reeve
    even them in?

        Into the snows she sweeps,
            Hurling the haven behind,
        The Deutschland, on Sunday; and so the sky keeps,
            For the infinite air is unkind,
    And the sea flint-flake, black-backed in the regular blow,
    Sitting Eastnortheast, in cursed quarter, the wind;
        Wiry and white-fiery and whirlwind-swivellèd snow
Spins to the widow-making unchilding unfathering deeps.

        She drove in the dark to leeward,
            She struck—not a reef or a rock
        But the combs of a smother of sand: night drew her
            Dead to the Kentish Knock;
    And she beat the bank down with her bows and the ride of her
        keel:
    The breakers rolled on her beam with ruinous shock;
        And canvas and compass, the whorl and the wheel
Idle for ever to waft her or wind her with, these she endured.

        Hope had grown grey hairs,
            Hope had mourning on,
        Trenched with tears, carved with cares,
            Hope was twelve hours gone:
    And frightful a nightfall folded rueful a day
    Nor rescue, only rocket and lightship, shone,
        And lives at last were washing away:
To the shrouds they took,—they shook in the hurling and
    horrible airs.

16

One stirred from the rigging to save
The wild woman-kind below.
With a rope's end round the man, handy and brave—
He was pitched to his death at a blow,
For all his dreadnought breast and braids of thew:
They could tell him for hours, dandled the to and fro
Through the cobbled foam-fleece. What could he do
With the burl of the fountains of air, buck and the flood of the
    wave?

17

They fought with God's cold—
And they could not and fell to the deck
(Crushed them) or water (and drowned them) or rolled
With the sea-romp over the wreck.
Night roared, with the heart-break hearing a heart-broke rabble,
The woman's wailing, the crying of child without check—
Till a lioness arose breasting the babble,
A prophetess towered in the tumult, a virginal tongue told.

18

Ah, touched in your bower of bone,
Are you! turned for an exquisite smart,
Have you! make words break from me here all alone,
Do you!—mother of being in me, heart.
O unteachably after evil, but uttering truth,
Why, tears! is it? tears; such a melting, a madrigal start!
Never-eldering revel and river of youth,
What can it be, this glee? the good you have there of your own?

19

Sister, a sister calling
A master, her master and mine!—
And the inboard seas run swirling and hawling;
The rash smart sloggering brine
Blinds her; but she that weather sees one thing, one;
Has one fetch in her: she rears herself to divine
Ears, and the call of the tall nun
To the men in the tops and the tackle rode over the storm's
    brawling.

20

She was first of a five and came
Of a coifèd sisterhood.
(O Deutschland, double a desperate name!
O world wide of its good!
But Gertrude, lily, and Luther, are two of a town,
Christ's lily and beast of the waste wood:
From life's dawn it is drawn down,
Abel is Cain's brother and breasts they have sucked the same.)

21

Loathed for a love men knew in them,
Banned by the land of their birth,
Rhine refused them, Thames would ruin them;
Surf, snow, river and earth
Gnashed: but thou art above, thou Orion of light;
Thy unchancelling poising palms were weighing the worth,
Thou martyr-master: in thy sight
Storm flakes were scroll-leaved flowers, lily showers—sweet
heaven was astrew in them.

22

Five! the finding and sake
And cipher of suffering Christ.
Mark, the mark is of man's make
And the word of it Sacrificed.
But he scores it in scarlet himself on his own bespoken,
Before-time-taken, dearest prizèd and priced—
Stigma, signal, cinquefoil token
For lettering of the lamb's fleece, ruddying of the rose-flake.

23

Joy fall to thee, father Francis,
Drawn to the Life that died;
With the gnarls of the nails in thee, niche of the lance, his
Lovescape crucified
And seal of his seraph-arrival! and these thy daughters
And five-livèd and leavèd favour and pride,
Are sisterly sealed in wild waters,
To bathe in his fall-gold mercies, to breathe in his all-fire glances.

24

Away in the loveable west,
On a pastoral forehead of Wales,
I was under a roof here, I was at rest,
And they the prey of the gales;
She to the black-about air, to the breaker, the thickly
Falling flakes, to the throng that catches and quails
Was calling 'O Christ, Christ, come quickly':
The cross to her she calls Christ to her, christens her wild-worst
Best.

25

The majesty! what did she mean?
Breathe, arch and original Breath.
Is it love in her of the being as her lover had been?
Breathe, body of lovely Death.
They were else-minded then, altogether, the men
Woke thee with a *We are perishing* in the weather of Gennesareth.
Or is it that she cried for the crown then,
The keener to come at the comfort for feeling the combating
keen?

26

For how to the heart's cheering
The down-dugged ground-hugged grey
Hovers off, the jay-blue heavens appearing
Of pied and peeled May!
Blue-beating and hoary-glow height; or night, still higher,
With belled fire and the moth-soft Milky Way,
What by your measure is the heaven of desire,
The treasure never eyesight got, nor was ever guessed what for
the hearing?

27

No, but it was not these.
The jading and jar of the cart,
Time's tasking, it is fathers that asking for ease
Of the sodden-with-its-sorrowing heart,
Not danger, electrical horror; then further it finds
The appealing of the Passion is tenderer in prayer apart:
Other, I gather, in measure her mind's
Burden, in wind's burly and beat of endragonèd seas.

28

But how shall I . . . make me room there:
Reach me a . . . Fancy, come faster—
Strike you the sight of it? look at it loom there,
Thing that she . . . There then! the Master,
Ipse, the only one, Christ, King, Head:
He was to cure the extremity where he had cast her;
Do, deal, lord it with living and dead;
Let him ride, her pride, in his triumph, despatch and have done
with his doom there.

Ah! there was a heart right!
There was single eye!
Read the unshapeable shock night
And knew the who and the why;
Wording it how but by him that present and past,
Heaven and earth are word of, worded by?—
The Simon Peter of a soul! to the blast
Tarpeïan-fast, but a blown beacon of light.

Jesu, heart's light,
Jesu, maid's son,
What was the feast followed the night
Thou hadst glory of this nun?—
Feast of the one woman without stain.
For so conceivèd, so to conceive thee is done;
But here was heart-throe, birth of a brain,
Word, that heard and kept thee and uttered thee outright.

Well, she has thee for the pain, for the
Patience; but pity of the rest of them!
Heart, go and bleed at a bitterer vein for the
Comfortless unconfessed of them—
No not uncomforted: lovely-felicitous Providence
Finger of a tender of, O of a feathery delicacy, the breast of the
Maiden could obey so, be a bell to, ring of it, and
Startle the poor sheep back! is the shipwrack then a harvest, does
tempest carry the grain for thee?

I admire thee, master of the tides,
　　Of the Yore-flood, of the year's fall;
　The recurb and the recovery of the gulf's sides,
　　　The girth of it and the wharf of it and the wall;
　Stanching, quenching ocean of a motionable mind;
　Ground of being, and granite of it: past all
　　Grasp God, throned behind
Death with a sovereignty that heeds but hides, bodes but
　　abides;

　　With a mercy that outrides
　　The all of water, an ark
　For the listener; for the lingerer with a love glides
　　Lower than death and the dark;
　A vein for the visiting of the past-prayer, pent in prison,
　The-last-breath penitent spirits—the uttermost mark
　　Our passion-plungèd giant risen,
The Christ of the Father compassionate, fetched in the storm
　　of his strides.

　　Now burn, new born to the world,
　　Doubled-naturèd name,
　The heaven-flung, heart-fleshed, maiden-furled
　　Miracle-in-Mary-of-flame,
　Mid-numberèd he in three of the thunder-throne!
　Not a dooms-day dazzle in his coming nor dark as he came;
　　Kind, but royally reclaiming his own;
A released shower, let flash to the shire, not a lightning of fire
　　hard-hurled.

　　Dame, at our door
　　Drowned, and among our shoals,
　Remember us in the roads, the heaven-haven of the
　　　reward:
　　Our King back, Oh, upon English souls!
　Let him easter in us, be a dayspring to the dimness of us, be a
　　crimson-cresseted east,
　More brightening her, rare-dear Britain, as his reign rolls,
　　Pride, rose, prince, hero of us, high-priest,
Our hearts' charity's hearth's fire, our thoughts' chivalry's
　　throng's Lord.

The Wreck of the Deutschland is Hopkins's first, and many would say his greatest, mature poem. We know, from his letter to R.W. Dixon of 5 October 1878, how he came to write it:

> When in the winter of '75 the *Deutschland* was wrecked in the mouth of the Thames and five Franciscan nuns, exiles from Germany by the Falck Laws, aboard of her were drowned I was affected by the account and happening to say so to my rector he said that he wished someone would write a poem on the subject. On this hint I set to work and, though my hand was out at first, produced one. I had long had haunting my ear the echo of a new rhythm which now I realized on paper . . .

Full reports of the wreck appeared in *The Times*, 8–13 December 1875: Hopkins had obviously read them.

The poem is at the same time clearly autobiographical: 'I may add for your greater interest and edification', Hopkins wrote to Bridges in August 1877, 'that what refers to myself in the poem is all strictly and literally true and did all occur; nothing is added for poetical padding.' Hopkins's own spiritual crisis (Part the First) is, then, as important to the poem as the shipwreck itself (Part the Second), and both are given meaning as symbols of Christ's suffering. The resultant unity, the binding together of shipwreck and spiritual struggle, is perhaps the poem's most impressive quality. As F.R. Leavis put it succinctly, in *New Bearings in English Poetry*, 'The wreck he describes is both occasion and symbol. He realizes it so vividly that he is in it; and it is at the same time in him.'

The poem's ultimate subject, then, is the paradox of suffering; or, as Hopkins put it in his notes on the *Spiritual Exercises*, 'the great sacrifice', the reliving of Christ's Passion and Crucifixion. The conviction that he could devote a poem to this all-important theme justified for him the breaking of his self-imposed seven years' silence. There were, of course, more specifically poetic reasons too: the desire to realize the 'new rhythm', on which he had been lecturing at Roehampton; the conviction that in poetry he could best express the inscapes which he now found everywhere in nature; the excitement of first reading classical Welsh poetry. The discovery, the year before, that Bridges had just published a volume of poems probably played a part too.

The Wreck of the Deutschland is thus not only a deeply personal religious poem, but a great technical achievement, full of the vitality of experiment. Difficulties, of course, there are: both subject-matter and innovations make it a highly complex poem. But they have been exaggerated. In his use of language Hopkins was going back to the great age of English poetry, to Shakespeare and the seventeenth-century poets: he was using words—the full resources of words— images and emblems, as the Metaphysical poets had used them. In

THE LOSS OF THE DEUTSCHLAND.

(FROM OUR OWN REPORTER.)

HARWICH, FRIDAY.

The bodies of the four German nuns were removed to-day for interment at a convent of the Franciscan order, to which they belonged, near Stratford. They were from a convent in Westphalia.

From the statements of survivors and evidence given by the captain and others, an account of the shipwreck was obtained, the first portion of which was published yesterday. What follows is the continuation of this narrative. Most of the passengers were awoke by the breaking of the screw when the ship struck. They hurriedly dressed and came on deck. The danger, however, did not then seem imminent, and the assurances of the captain and his officers, added to the intense cold and wet, soon sent them shivering alarmed below. At first some sail was set. The cargo in the forehold was thrown overboard. The male passengers were summoned at daylight on Monday to man the pumps, and worked at them cheerily. After some hours' work, however, the vessel made so much water that Captain Brickenstein feared if she slipped off the bank into deep water she would go down like a stone. He therefore anchored. The boats were at first ordered to be cleared away, and the story of one who got away and was borne to Sheerness is already known. It was the captain's opinion, however, that no boats could live in such a sea, and he had confident hopes of a speedy rescue. After daylight the remaining serviceable boats were not used. They were, I believe, three in number, including a life boat. And now comes the most remarkable and pitiable chapter in a sad story. Rockets were thrown up directly the Deutschland struck; in the blinding snowstorm, however, they no doubt were invisible to the lightships. But Monday was a tolerably clear day; passing vessels were distinctly seen from the Deutschland's deck, and every effort was made to attract their intention. The passengers and crew watched those vessels, two of them steamers, hoping that each one of them had seen, or must soon seen, the signal of distress. But one after another passed by and night came on. All this time the passengers had not suffered materially. It is possible that a few may have been washed overboard as they first hurried on deck after the vessel struck. But after the first shock they kept up their spirits well. Plenty to eat and drink was served out to them, and the work to which the male passengers were put was useful in diverting their thoughts, but it became known that at night the rising tide and rough sea would imperil all on board. At night, therefore, rockets were thrown up once more, and this time they were answered from the Sunk Light, a lightship to the south-east of the wreck. The signals at the Sunk Light were repeated by the men at the Cork Lightship, which is situated still near to Harwich, and after some time they were answered by the Coastguard at Harwich. But there is no lifeboat at Harwich, and whether from this cause or not, although on Monday night it was known at Harwich that a vessel was in distress, no help was tendered till daylight on Tuesday morning. Some of the jury on Thursday expressed the belief that if a lifeboat had been stationed it might have been towed out to sea by the steam tug, and the two together might have saved the lives of nearly all on board the wreck. I have talked with the captain of the steam tug, who is represented to me, and no doubt is, a brave fellow, ready to risk his life in any hopeful enterprise. But the Kentish Knock is 25 miles distant from Harwich, and the wreck is 27 miles distant. The Knock is approached from here by a difficult navigation, and Carrington, the captain of the tug, says that in thick weather, with such a sea as was running on Monday night the task of rescuing life at such a distance would have been hopeless even with a lifeboat. I have no doubt both these theories will be amply discussed hereafter. It is sad anyhow to know that these 200 fellow-creatures remained for some 30 hours so close to the English coast, passed by English vessels during the day, and their signals of distress seen and answered from the land at night, and that, notwithstanding, so many of them perished just at the last. I said that their situation first became perilous on Monday night or rather Tuesday morning. At 2 a.m., Captain Brickenstein, knowing that with the rising tide the ship would be waterlogged, ordered all the passengers to come on deck. Danger levels class distinctions, and steerage and first-class passengers were by this time together in the after saloon and cabins. Most of them obeyed the summons at once; others lingered below till it was too late; some of them, ill, weak, despairing of life even on deck, resolved to stay in their cabins and meet death without any further struggle to evade it. After 3 a.m. on Tuesday morning a scene of horror was witnessed. Some passengers clustered for safety within or upon the wheelhouse, and on the top of other slight structures on deck. Most of the crew and many of the emigrants went into the rigging, where they were safe enough as long as they could maintain their hold. But the intense cold and long exposure told a tale. The purser of the ship, though a strong man, relaxed his grasp, and fell into the sea. Women and children and men were one by one swept away from their shelters on the deck. Five German nuns, whose bodies are now in the dead-house here, clasped hands and were drowned together, the chief sister, a gaunt woman 6ft. high, calling out loudly and often "O Christ, come quickly!" till the end came. The shrieks and sobbing of women and children are described by the survivors as agonizing. One brave sailor, who was safe in the rigging, went down to try and save a child or woman who was drowning on deck. He was secured by a rope to the rigging, but a wave dashed him against the bulwarks, and when daylight dawned his headless body, detained by the rope, was seen swaying to and fro with the waves. In the dreadful excitement of these hours one man hung himself behind the wheelhouse, another hacked at his wrist with a knife, hoping to die a comparatively painless death by bleeding. It was nearly 8 o'clock before the tide and sea abated, and the survivors could venture to go on deck. At half-past 10 o'clock the tugboat from Harwich came alongside and brought all away without further accident. Most of the passengers are German emigrants, and it is only right to add that they have received here from the first the utmost kindness and sympathy.

Parts of stanzas 16, 19 and 24 of Hopkins's The Wreck of the Deutschland *are based on this report.*

his use of sprung rhythm (here used for the first time) he was aiming at the maximum stress or emphasis, to reflect the stress, the struggle, of what the poem told; to 'fetch out' the meaning, as he put it. The poem is an ode, but a highly dramatic ode; and the sprung rhythm contributes forcefully to the drama. To repeat the explanation of it Hopkins gave to Dixon: 'To speak shortly, it consists in scanning by accents or stresses alone, without any account of the number of syllables, so that a foot may be one strong syllable or it may be many light and one strong.' That could hardly be simpler; and it gave him, as he said, much greater freedom than ordinary syllabic rhythm.

In Part the First the distribution of stresses in each eight-line stanza is 2–3–4–3–5–5–4–6; in Part the Second the first line has three stresses. Originally, Hopkins told Dixon, he 'had to mark the stresses in blue chalk' (this was one of the reasons, he said, why the *Month* 'dared not print' the poem). Both the surviving MSS carry some stressmarks; and by relying on the normal strength of words and syllables, and on Hopkins's favourite devices—alliteration, assonance, internal rhyming and 'chiming' of consonants—we can be confident of where the stresses fall. We can also see how they 'fetch out' the meaning. The scanning of, for example, Stanza 3 brings home to us strongly the mixed terror and joy of the spiritual experience Hopkins describes (Christopher Devlin has argued convincingly that it was not, as many have thought, his conversion, but his experience of a particular Exercise during his first Long Retreat as a novice at Roehampton):

> The frówn of his fáce
> Befóre me, the húrtle of héll
> Behínd, whére, whére was a, whére was a place?
> I whírled out wíngs that spéll
> And fléd with a flíng of the heárt to the heárt of the Hóst.
> My heárt, but you were dóvewínged, Í can téll,
> Cárrier-wítted, I am bóld to bóast,
> To flásh from the fláme to the fláme then, tówer from the gráce
> to the gráce.

Other devices add their weight to the stressing: the alliteration and assonance; the three-times repeated 'where' in line 3 that wonderfully 'fetches out' the terror and lostness; the development of the image of the poet's heart as a bird, from panic-stricken flight to homing to poised and graceful soaring.

Bridges advised readers of Hopkins's poems to leave *The Wreck of the Deutschland* until last; but, apart from its major interest as spiritual autobiography, it anticipates all the major themes of Hopkins's mature poetry, even hinting at the desolation of the final Dublin sonnets. And it already shows full command of his most brilliant, individual effects: intense inscapes of nature and feeling ('I kiss my hand/To the stars, lovely-asunder/Starlight, wafting him out of it': Stanza 5); and daring metaphysical images: the hourglass and mountain-stream of Stanza 4, the Incarnation riding time 'like riding a river' of Stanza 6, Christ as 'Our passion-plungèd giant', 'fetched in the storm of his strides', of Stanza 33.

It remains, nevertheless, the most difficult of Hopkins's major poems, and a short descriptive summary, however inadequate to its richness, may be of some help.

Part the First (Stanza 1–10) has almost the shape of a fugue. The two key subjects are God's mastery and His mercy: the first introduced dramatically and personally in the poem's first line ('Thou mastering me/God!') and developing through dread and terror to the crisis halfway through Stanza 3; the second, the haven offered by Christ in the Sacrament, taking over for the rest of that stanza. This is Hopkins's own 'shipwreck' and salvation. Both subjects are enriched in the next two stanzas: Hopkins's 'soft sift/In an hourglass' is steadied by 'Christ's gift'; in return, he experiences God's mystery through the beauty and glory of His works. The next three stanzas, the most concentrated and perhaps most difficult of the poem, bring the two subjects together in the paradox of Christ's Incarnation and Passion: it is both eternal ('But it rides time like riding a river') and historical ('It dates from day/Of his going in Galilee'); in death it offers life ('Warm-laid grave of a womb-life grey': a marvellous example of the Welsh *cynghanedd* in its 'chiming' of sounds); and it demands acceptance, like a sloe bursting in our mouth and flushing us 'sour or sweet,/Brim, in a flash, full!'

Stanzas 9 and 10 complete the fugue and further deepen the central paradox:

> Thou art lightning and love, I found it, a winter and warm;
> Father and fondler of heart thou hast wrung.

They also look forward to Part II in the asking for 'wrecking and storm', the fulfilment of God's paradoxical purpose.

Part the Second (Stanzas 11 to the end) is divided between the narrative of the shipwreck and apparent digressions (which are in fact fused with the poem's total meaning); it ends with a return to the theme of Part I.

Stanza 11 introduces, with all Hopkins's power of alliteration and 'chiming', the inevitability of death:

> The sour scythe cringe, and the blear share come.

The sailing out and the wreck itself occupy only the next six stanzas, with a return to 'the tall nun' calling in the storm in Stanza

19: they are faithful to the account in *The Times*, yet, in the movement, sound and look of the words, give a remarkable sense of the storm and wreck as an apocalyptic disaster:

> And the sea flint-flake, black-backed in the regular blow . . .
> Wiry and white-fiery and whirlwind-swivellèd snow . . .

After the dramatic introduction of the tall nun at the end of Stanza 17, comes the first 'digression', as Hopkins turns to his own heart, itself feeling both grief and joy at the sight. The paradox of that relates the stanza to the theme of the whole poem. Some have found the next four stanzas (20–23) on the nuns' birthplace and their dedication to St Francis of Assisi purely decorative or even irrelevant. But for Hopkins everything contributes to 'the great sacrifice', the paradox that suffering brings salvation: the nuns' exile from Germany, their martyrdom in the wreck, even their number, five. All mirror the life of St Francis, whose dedication to Christ earned him the five stigmata.

Stanza 24 gives us the tall nun's call in the storm, 'O Christ, Christ, come quickly': made keener by the glance at his own comfort in Wales. It is the centre of the poem; but the real climax comes four stanzas later, in Stanza 28, when Hopkins gives us the *meaning* of the call, the vision that had inspired it. The three stanzas in between prepare for its true, all but inexpressible meaning, by rejecting the alternatives. Did she wish to become more like the suffering Christ herself? No, we know from the story of Lake Gennesareth that even Christ's disciples were terrified of drowning then. Or did she wish to suffer more keenly to win a greater martyr's crown in heaven? For we know that the beauty of heaven surpasses all our senses (Stanza 26). No, it was not the sudden horror of the storm that made her ask for ease; but the day-by-day burden of a life of self-sacrifice ('The jading and jar of the cart,/ . . . the sodden-with-its sorrowing heart'). Stanza 28 gives us the true meaning of the call; the ellipses show that it is virtually inexpressible. The nun's vision is of Christ Himself (*'Ipse'*), physically present, walking across the waves of the sea. He will, as Master, take her to Him. Stanzas 29 and 30 complete the triumph of the nun: she has comprehended the terrible storm aright; in uttering the Word, 'Christ', she has given birth to Him just as Mary had done: hence the significance of the night of the storm being the eve of the Feast of the Immaculate Conception (8 December).

Stanza 31 turns to the plight of the other passengers, the 'Comfortless unconfessed'. But here too is a miracle: for, providentially, the nun's cry has rung out like a bell to startle the lost sheep back to the fold; is not the 'shipwrack' then a harvest? It is this miracle that leads Hopkins to praise God in the next two stanzas for His mastery and His mercy, the two qualities for which He was adored in Part the First of the poem.

The last two stanzas, befitting a great religious ode, are prayer: first to Christ, to 'burn' with flame anew, having mercifully—but 'royally'—reclaimed His own in the wreck; and finally to the nun, 'Dame, at our door/Drowned', to intercede for us in heaven, to beg the return of Christ to England, 'rare-dear Britain' (in Hopkins's eyes, heretical since the Reformation). The poem ends on a crescendo of worship for Christ.

> Our hearts' charity's hearth's fire, our thoughts' chivalry's
> throng's Lord,

in which the perfect balance and interlacing of vowels, consonants and words is a microcosm of the interlocking and unity of the whole ode.

The Starlight Night

Look at the stars! look, look up at the skies!
  O look at all the fire-folk sitting in the air!
  The bright boroughs, the circle-citadels there!
Down in dim woods the diamond delves! the elves'-eyes!
The grey lawns cold where gold, where quickgold lies!
  Wind-beat whitebeam! airy abeles set on a flare!
  Flake-doves sent floating forth at a farmyard scare!—
Ah well! it is all a purchase, all is a prize.

Buy then! bid then!—What?—Prayer, patience, alms, vows.
Look, look: a May-mess, like on orchard boughs!
  Look! March-bloom, like on mealed-with-yellow sallows!
These are indeed the barn; withindoors house
The shocks. This piece-bright paling shuts the spouse
  Christ home, Christ and his mother and all his hallows.

The Starlight Night is the second of the ten sonnets Hopkins wrote in 1877, his final year at St Beuno's, leading up to his ordination in September. It is dated 24 February, the day after *God's Grandeur*; Hopkins sent both sonnets to Bridges that April. Like all these sonnets, it celebrates nature; or rather, it celebrates Christ as the creator of nature. In writing it, Hopkins has carried out the opening exercise of the *Spiritual Exercises*: 'Man was created to praise . . .' The octet not only gives us the beauty of the star-world, it insists that we experience it excitedly and anew:

> Look at the stars! look, look up at the skies!
>   O look at all the fire-folk sitting in the air!

The repeated imperatives and exclamations communicate the excitement; as does Hopkins's use of a 'sprung' line for the sonnet's opening:

Lóok at the/stárs!/lóok, look,/úp at the/skíes!

Here the stresses emphasize, 'fetch out' the meaning; just as they do in the first line of the sestet, the only other 'sprung' line:

Búy then!/bíd then!—What?—/Práyer, pátience, alms,/vóws.

Besides the beauty of the stars, the octet gives us their mysterious order ('bright boroughs', 'circle-citadels'); their pre-dawn magic ('The grey lawns cold'); the sense we have of their movement, like rippling leaves or doves in flight. The sestet is equally insistent on how we may possess such beauty: through action, Christian devotion. Then, with a remarkable leap of thought, Hopkins makes us see that even all this beauty is only external, 'the barn', 'the paling' (or fence): the *true* beauty, the harvest (the 'shocks' or stooks of grain), is within: Christ and His Mother and all the saints. It is this, then, that lies behind the beauty and order and mystery of the star-world, that we must make our own with our prayers. That leap from stars to 'paling' goes back to a fragment Hopkins had written in his undergraduate diary nearly twelve years before:

> The stars were packed so close that night
> They seemed to press and stare
> And gather in like hurdles bright
> The liberties of air.

It shows something of the fermentation that had clearly gone on during his poetic silence.

The Windhover:

To Christ our Lord

I caught this morning morning's minion, king-
  dom of daylight's dauphin, dapple-dawn-drawn Falcon, in
    his riding
Of the rolling level underneath him steady air, and striding
High there, how he rung upon the rein of a wimpling wing
In his ecstasy! then off, off forth on swing,
  As a skate's heel sweeps smooth on a bow-bend: the hurl and
    gliding
Rebuffed the big wind. My heart in hiding
Stirred for a bird,—the achieve of, the mastery of the thing!

Brute beauty and valour and act, oh, air, pride, plume, here
    Buckle! AND the fire that breaks from thee then, a billion
Times told lovelier, more dangerous, O my chevalier!

    No wonder of it: shéer plód makes plough down sillion
Shine, and blue-bleak embers, ah my dear,
    Fall, gall themselves, and gash gold-vermilion.

Hopkins dated his corrected version of *The Windhover*, to which he
added the dedication to Christ, St Beuno's, 30 May 1877. He later
described it to Bridges as 'the best thing I ever wrote'. The poem has
been more discussed and interpreted than any other Hopkins poem,
but almost all critics have agreed on its greatness. It is essential to
keep the dedication in mind. Both *The Starlight Night* and *Hurrahing
in Harvest* have Christ explicitly as subject: He is the presence found
in the beauty of stars or the beauty of harvest and hills. Christ is
not mentioned in *The Windhover*, except in the dedication. The
kestrel in its flight is the most superbly and sustainedly observed of
all Hopkins's natural phenomena; but the imagery throughout
makes it clear that it is also a symbol of Christ's beauty and the sonnet
an act of acceptance of the life of sacrifice.

    The octet, in its rhythm and almost breathless, but controlled,
excitement, wonderfully imitates the kestrel's soaring and gliding
flight. Images from chivalry, the riding-school and skating, add to
the bird's grace and power. But the chivalric images ('minion . . .
Kingdom . . . dauphin') also draw on the great meditation on the
Kingdom of Christ in the *Spiritual Exercises*: Christ is the supreme
Chevalier; the Jesuit priest (which Hopkins was so soon to be) is
Christ's soldier. 'I caught' is the mental seizing of inscape: both of
the kestrel and of Christ, whose presence Hopkins sees in the bird's
'achieve of, the mastery of the thing!' Why 'My heart in hiding' at
the end of the octet? Some critics, notably William Empson and
I.A. Richards, have explained it as Hopkins's envy for the more
dangerous life of the kestrel, for the life of the senses and 'mortal
beauty'. These is certainly an element of that in a sonnet that
embodies—and ultimately solves—a spiritual conflict. But the tone
is surely more of wry acceptance. Hopkins has dedicated himself
to Christ's service, to the 'hidden life' (in a sermon he refers to 'the
hidden life at Nazareth' as 'the great help to faith').

    The crux of the poem comes in the first three lines of the sextet,
in the meaning and tense of the word *buckle*. Its commonest meaning
is 'collapse, give way under strain'. If this is the meaning Hopkins
intended, then the tense is indicative; the gliding kestrel has dived
down, and the three lines can be paraphrased: 'The beauty and
grace and power of your plumage crumple and bend as you swoop
down; and the light that flashes from you then is a billion times

The Vale of Clwyd

lovelier and more daring than before, my chevalier!' The lines obliquely refer to the life of sacrifice that Hopkins has accepted; and, ultimately, to Christ's own sacrifice for men. But, as critics have pointed out, the kestrel dives for its prey; its wings, although held tight to its body, do *not* crumple as it dives; it is at its deadliest and most controlled as it seizes its victim. *Buckle* has two older meanings, both found frequently in the Authorized Version of the Bible and in Shakespeare: (*a*) 'grapple, prepare for action' (*intransitive*), and (*b*) 'fasten, buckle on' (*transitive*). In both of these possible meanings the tense is imperative. The kestrel does not dive; its 'Brute beauty and valour and act' are the qualities of its soaring and gliding, so powerfully shown in the octet. In (*a*), the cry is to the kestrel's qualities themselves: 'Oh, beauty and grace, pride and plumage of the kestrel, come to my heart and prepare for action there! And the light that will flash from you [my heart] then will be a billion times lovelier and more daring, my heart become kestrel/chevalier!' In (*b*), the cry is to Christ: 'Oh, buckle on, fasten to my heart the beauty and grace, pride and plumage of the kestrel! And the light . . . !'

It is, I think, impossible to be certain that any one of these meanings totally excludes the other two. William Empson, indeed, in *Seven Types of Ambiguity*, sees the poem as one of unconscious friction, where the ambiguity expresses two incompatible ways of life, each intensely desired. But the final three lines make it clear that, whatever the conflict, Hopkins accepts the life of sacrifice; and this must support the first meaning of *buckle* as 'collapse'. The two key images here link with 'the fire' of line 10: they illustrate, from the homeliest experience, that the heart dedicated to service and sacrifice shines brightest. The plodding horse makes the ploughshare gleam down the furrow (*sillion*); and the cold-blue embers of a dying fire, as they fall, break apart and blaze out golden and red. 'Fall, gall themselves, and gash' strongly suggests the Crucifixion; 'ah my dear', taken from George Herbert's *Love* (2) ('Ah, my dear,/I cannot look on Thee'), and addressed to Christ, shows the strength and poignancy of Hopkins's desire, in his own life, to imitate Him. Many years later he wrote to Dixon: 'Christ our Lord . . . was doomed to succeed by failure.'

Hurrahing in Harvest

Summer ends now; now, barbarous in beauty, the stooks rise
    Around; up above, what wind-walks! what lovely behaviour
    Of silk-sack clouds! has wilder, wilful-wavier
Meal-drift moulded ever and melted across skies?

I walk, I lift up, I lift up heart, eyes,
    Down all that glory in the heavens to glean our Saviour;
    And, éyes, heárt, what looks, what lips yet gave you a
Rapturous love's greeting of realer, of rounder replies?

And the azurous hung hills are his world-wielding shoulder
    Majestic—as a stallion stalwart, very-violet-sweet!—
These things, these things were here and but the beholder
    Wanting; which two when they once meet,
The heart rears wings bold and bolder
    And hurls for him, O half hurls earth for him off under his feet.

Hurrahing in Harvest is dated 'Vale of Clwyd, 1 September 1877'. It was the outcome, Hopkins wrote to Bridges, 'of half an hour of extreme enthusiasm as I walked home alone one day from fishing in the Elwy'. It is perhaps the most ecstatic of this group of celebratory poems: it celebrates a direct vision of Christ's physical presence in nature, and it does so in one of Hopkins's boldest and most original images, 'as a stallion stalwart, very-violet-sweet!' The conjunction there, the strength of the stallion, and the sweetness of the violet, to express Christ's paradoxically double nature, 'explodes' on us, as Hopkins said poetry should. The whole poem, like *The Windhover*, is in 'sprung' rhythm, with many 'outriding' feet, that is syllables not counted in the scanning (marked by Hopkins in his MS): the resultant sound is an intimate part of the sonnet's excitement.

In the first four lines, Hopkins merges two of his favourite inscapes, the beauty of harvest and the beauty of the autumn clouds: 'barbarous' is peculiarly rich, bringing together the bearded corn and the wild beauty of the stooks; 'Meal-drift' identifies grain and cloud. The rapturous experience of all this gives him the vision of Christ's physical presence in the corn-fields ('glean' has the double meaning of gathering corn and gathering facts, here, *the* fact, Christ); and the hills surrounding the Vale of Clwyd chime in with their further evidence of Christ's physical majesty. 'Azurous' has a haunting beauty of sound; but it is precise too: blue was the colour that had first struck Hopkins in the Vale of Clwyd—'blue bloom, like meal', he had noted in his Journal.

The vision itself, the coming together in the sonnet's last four lines of Christ's presence and the poet, is one of the finest examples, in all Hopkins, of 'instress', the force exerted on the beholder by inscape, here, the supreme inscape. Hopkins's image for what happens reminds us of *The Windhover*: the heart 'réars wíngs' (Hopkins put in the stress-marks); it 'hurls' (Hopkins's favourite verb) the world away from the experiencer in his ecstasy. Meditation has become pure and active vision.

Henry Purcell

The poet wishes well to the divine genius of Purcell and praises him that, whereas other musicians have given utterance to the moods of man's mind, he has, beyond that, uttered in notes the very make and species of man as created both in him and in all men generally.

Have fair fallen, O fair, fair have fallen, so dear
To me, so arch-especial a spirit as heaves in Henry Purcell,
An age is now since passed, since parted; with the reversal
Of the outward sentence low lays him, listed to a heresy, here.

Not mood in him nor meaning, proud fire or sacred fear,
Or love or pity or all that sweet notes not his might nursle:
It is the forgèd feature finds me; it is the rehearsal
Of own, of abrúpt sélf there so thrusts on, so throngs the ear.

Let him oh! with his air of angels then lift me, lay me! only I'll
Have an eye to the sakes of him, quaint moonmarks, to his
        pelted plumage under
Wings: so some great stormfowl, whenever he has walked his
        while

The thunder-purple seabeach plumèd purple-of-thunder,
If a wuthering of his palmy snow-pinions scatter a colossal smile
Off him, but meaning motion fans fresh our wits with wonder.

Henry Purcell was the third of the nine poems Hopkins wrote during the ten months, December 1878 to October 1879, he spent as a priest at St Aloysius's Church, Oxford. It is dated April 1879. Although the sonnet written immediately before it, *Duns Scotus's Oxford*, shows his disillusion with what the nineteenth century has done to Oxford ('Thou hast a base and brickish skirt there, sours/ That neighbour-nature thy grey beauty is grounded/Best in;'), Oxford, with its memories, still retained a very special place in Hopkins's affections; and this stay was poetically very fruitful to him. *Henry Purcell* is one of his finest, most rewarding sonnets ('one of my very best pieces', he told Bridges); it has also great interest on several other counts. It was the first sonnet he wrote in Alexandrines, six-feet lines, with a stress to each foot: the complexity of the thought certainly needed the longer metre. It is a difficult sonnet, in grammar as well as thought; and, because Bridges was constantly asking for explanations of it over the next four years, we have more of Hopkins's annotation of this sonnet than of any other of his poems. We know precisely what he meant by almost every word. And, finally, to Hopkins, himself a musician if an amateur one, Purcell's music was the very essence of music, 'something necessary and eternal'—like Milton's verse, as he wrote to Dixon. More than that, Hopkins experienced in Purcell's music, as his prose argument at the head of the poem makes clear, the inscape, the *haecceitas* ('thisness'), the very selfhood of man: so that the sonnet celebrates not only Purcell himself, but 'selfhood', the principle of individuation that Hopkins had learnt from Duns Scotus.

It seems best to begin with Hopkins's precise explanation of the sonnet to Bridges, in a letter of 4 January 1883:

> The sonnet on Purcell means this: 1–4. I hope Purcell is not damned for being a Protestant, because I love his genius. 5–8. And that not so much for gifts he shares, even though it should be in higher measure, with other musicians as for his own individuality. 9–14. So that while he is aiming only at impressing me his hearer with the meaning in hand I am looking out meanwhile for his specific, his individual markings and mottlings, 'the sakes of him'. It is as when a bird thinking only of soaring spreads its wings: a beholder may happen then to have his attention drawn by the act to the plumage displayed.

Much earlier, he had told Bridges more shortly: 'My sonnet means "Purcell's music is none of your d—d subjective rot" (so to speak). Read it again.'

Hopkins's explanation still leaves difficulties: as they are solved, the sonnet's daring beauties, musical and linguistic, fall into place. The opening line offers one: Hopkins had to explain to Bridges that 'Have fair fallen' means 'May fair fortune have befallen'.

This is a terrible business about my sonnet 'Have fair fallen'. *Have* . . . is the singular imperative (or optative if you like) of the past. . . . As in the second person we say 'Have done' . . ., so one can say in the third person not only 'Fair fall' of what is present or future but also 'Have fair fallen' of what is past.

Hopkins's prayer for Purcell continues in the last clause of this first section: 'May the condemnation under which he outwardly or nominally lay for being out of the true Church (enlisted to a heresy) have been reversed.' 'Arch-especial', Hopkins's word for a thing's or person's selfhood, looks forward to the most individual quality of Purcell's genius that Hopkins celebrates:

> It is the forgèd feature finds me; it is the rehearsal
> Of own, of abrúpt sélf there so thrusts on, so throngs the ear.

'Forgèd' has the force of the anvil; 'rehearsal' both its musical meaning and its more personal meaning of telling of oneself; 'throngs' links the experience with the important passage on self-hood, 'this throng and stack of being', in Hopkins's opening note on 'The Principle or Foundation' in the *Spiritual Exercises*.

In finding an exact analogue in the sestet for 'the forgèd feature', the genius of Purcell's music, Hopkins created one of the most majestic—and startling—of all his images: the 'great stormfowl', walking beside the sea and then soaring above it. *Sakes* is a key word: 'It is the *sake* of "for the sake of", *forsake, namesake, keepsake*', he explained to Bridges. 'In this case it is, as the sonnet says, distinctive quality in genius'; *moonmarks* are the 'crescent shaped markings on the quill-feathers' of the bird, he told him; and *wuthering* (*cf. Wuthering Heights*) 'a Northcountry word for the noise and rush of wind'. To get its full effect, the sestet must be read aloud, 'performed', as Hopkins frequently said his poems must be; and the voice must carry the subject of the last four lines, the 'great stormfowl', over the time-clause, the conditional clause and the subsidiary clause (*but* = 'only', 'simply'), to its main verb, 'fans fresh'. 'The sestet', Hopkins wrote to Bridges on 26 May 1879, the month after writing the sonnet, 'is not so clearly worked out as I could wish', and he gave him a very detailed and precise exposition of it. But its essential meaning comes out in the summary he gave him later, quoted above. The analogue is exact: the stormfowl, in soaring up, shows you unawares his distinctive beauty; Purcell, in his music, does the same. But to the beauty of the exact analogy is added Hopkins's marvellous visual sense; and to that his unique skill in making repeated and 'chiming' sounds echo the majesty of the imagined scene:

> The thunder-purple seabeach, plumèd purple-of-thunder.

Felix Randal

Felix Randal the farrier, O he is dead then? my duty all ended,
Who have watched his mould of man, big-boned and hardy-
    handsome
Pining, pining, till time when reason rambled in it and some
Fatal four disorders, fleshed there, all contended?

Sickness broke him. Impatient he cursed at first, but mended
Being anointed and all; though a heavenlier heart began some
Months earlier, since I had our sweet reprieve and ransom
Tendered to him. Ah well, God rest him all road ever he
    offended!

This seeing the sick endears them to us, us too it endears.
My tongue had taught thee comfort, touch had quenched thy
    tears,
Thy tears that touched my heart, child, Felix, poor Felix
    Randal;

How far from then forethought of, all thy more boisterous years,
When thou at the random grim forge, powerful amidst peers,
Didst fettle for the great grey drayhorse his bright and battering
    sandal!

Hopkins served as a parish priest at St Francis Xavier's, Liverpool, a slum parish, from the end of December 1879 until early August 1881, nearly twenty months: his longest assignment to such work. He was appalled by the conditions, moral and physical; indeed, Bridges wrote that 'the vice and horrors nearly killed him'. Apologizing to Bridges for not writing, he gave way to a fit of despair: 'One is so fagged, so harried and gallied up and down. And the drunkards go on drinking, the filthy, as the scripture says, are filthy still: human nature is inveterate. Would that I had seen the last of it.' Not surprisingly, he found the writing of poetry extremely difficult: 'Liverpool is of all places the most museless', he wrote to Dixon. Nevertheless, he wrote three poems there, all in 1880: *Felix Randal* on 28 April, *Brothers* in August and *Spring and Fall* on 7 September.

There are clearly some affinities between *Felix Randal* and *Henry Purcell*. Both explore through an individual a distinctive quality that Hopkins cherishes in all men: selfhood, 'the very make' of man, in *Henry Purcell*, penitence, the 'heavenlier heart' in *Felix Randal*; both are in Alexandrines, in a sprung and outriding rhythm that contributes intimately to each sonnet's very different tone; *Felix Randal* ends with a memory of 'the great grey drayhorse' that, in its sound and splendid visual presence, to some extent matches the 'some great stormfowl' of *Henry Purcell*. But there the resemblances end. *Felix Randal* is, in its octet, a moving elegy on a blacksmith who has just died: Fr Alfred Thomas has discovered that he was, in fact, one of Hopkins's Liverpool flock. It recounts what Hopkins, as priest, has done for his last days and hours. More powerfully than any other of his poems, it brings together priest and poet. It is a peculiarly honest poem in two special respects: it shows clearly Hopkins's attraction to the man, 'big-boned and hardy-handsome', 'powerful amidst peers'—an attraction that becomes love, when, at the end, Felix needs Hopkins's love; and it shows equally clearly how a priest's ministrations add to his own sense of worth ('us too it endears'). The first three lines of the sestet, with their change to direct address of Felix, and their repetition of 'endears', 'touch', and 'tears', show how the consolation of the sonnet goes both ways: to Felix and to Hopkins himself. It is this consolation and sense of love, of worth, that lets the sonnet end on a note of near-elation, with its marvellously boisterous, physical memory of Felix in his prime:

> When thou at the random grim forge, powerful amidst peers,
> Didst fettle for the great grey drayhorse his bright and battering
>   sandal!

This sense of Felix's day-to-day life, enhanced as it is in that last line, is brought nearer by Hopkins's use of Lancashire dialect: *and all, all road ever* ('in whatever way'), *fettle* ('prepare').

Inversnaid

> This darksome burn, horseback brown,
> His rollrock highroad roaring down,
> In coop and in comb the fleece of his foam
> Flutes and low to the lake falls home.
>
> A windpuff-bonnet of fáwn-fróth
> Turns and twindles over the broth
> Of a pool so pitchblack, féll-frówning,
> It rounds and rounds Despair to drowning.
>
> Degged with dew, dappled with dew
> Are the groins of the braes that the brook treads through,
> Wiry heathpacks, flitches of fern,
> And the beadbonny ash that sits over the burn.
>
> What would the world be, once bereft
> Of wet and of wildness? Let them be left,
> O let them be left, wildness and wet;
> Long live the weeds and the wilderness yet.

Inversnaid Falls

Hopkins wrote *Inversnaid* on a short visit to the Scottish Highlands,
made from Glasgow in the autumn of 1881. The poem is dated 28
September. Inversnaid is the name of a burn (or brook) which flows
into Loch Lomond. The quick, almost rollicking, flow of the couplets,

and the impact of fresh, unusual words, make it one of Hopkins's happiest poems. Some of the words are Scottish, some archaic, some newly-coined; but all are remarkably exact in conjuring up the swift brook and the heather-covered hills it flows through. *Twindles* in line 6 is either Hopkins's compound of 'twists', 'twitches' and 'dwindles' (supported by a *Journal* entry: 'the foam dwindling and twitched into long chains of suds'), or a verb meaning 'splits into two parts' (from the archaic noun, *twindle*, a twin): it works either way. Two other coined compounds work particularly well too in 'inscaping' the landscape in the minimum number of words: *heathpacks*, clumps of heather; and *beadbonny*, of the ash (a tree that Hopkins especially loved), beautiful with its beadlike berries.

But the poem is not simply a description of the brook. It ends with a plea to let this wild beauty remain:

> What would the world be, once bereft
> Of wet and of wildness? Let them be left,
> O let them be left, wildness and wet;
> Long live the weeds and the wilderness yet.

The key words there had clearly been haunting Hopkins for over two years, since in February 1879 he had written to Bridges from Oxford that he had

something, if I cd. only seize it, on the decline of wild nature, beginning somehow like this—

> O where is it, the wilderness,
> The wildness of the wilderness?
> Where is it, the wilderness?

and ending—

> And wander in the wilderness;
> In the weedy wilderness,
> Wander in the wilderness.

The poignancy of the last stanza of *Inversnaid* goes, then, with Hopkins's fear in *Ribblesdale*, written in Lancashire the following year, that man will despoil nature's beauty, 'thriftless reave . . . our rich round world bare'; just as in *God's Grandeur* (1877) he had seen God's world wear 'man's smudge' and share 'man's smell'. This mood may help to explain the suddenly (and surprisingly) menacing image at the end of stanza 2:

> Of a pool so pitchblack, féll-frówning,
> It rounds and rounds Despair to drowning.

The whirlpool drowns despair; but the possibility of the changed mood is, if only briefly, acknowledged.

'As kingfishers catch fire'

As kingfishers catch fire, dragonflies draw flame;
As tumbled over rim in roundy wells
Stones ring; like each tucked string tells, each hung bell's
Bow swung finds tongue to fling out broad its name;
Each mortal thing does one thing and the same:
Deals out that being indoors each one dwells;
Selves—goes itself; *myself* it speaks and spells;
Crying *What I do is me: for that I came.*

I say more: the just man justices;
Kéeps gráce: thát keeps all his goings graces;
Acts in God's eye what in God's eye he is—
Christ. For Christ plays in ten thousand places,
Lovely in limbs, and lovely in eyes not his
To the Father through the features of men's faces.

This sonnet was given neither title nor date by Hopkins; but there are two passages in his spiritual notes, both probably of December 1881, strikingly similar to its theme and imagery. In the first he wrote: 'It is as if a man said: That is Christ playing at me and me playing at Christ, only it is no play but truth: That is Christ *being me* and me being Christ'; and in the second: 'All things therefore are charged with love, are charged with God and if we know how to touch them give off sparks and take fire, yield drops and flow, ring and tell of him.'

The sonnet is the clearest statement in all Hopkins's poems of Duns Scotus's belief in the fulfilling of individuality, in 'selving' (Hopkins's word). All created things, animate and even inanimate, exist to fulfil their own distinctive natures; in this way they praise God; and man's fulfilment of his nature finds perfection in Christ's Incarnation. In the first four lines visual beauty passes to sound; and Hopkins uses all his skills of alliteration, 'chiming' and assonance, to vary the individual vibrations of ringing stones, plucked (*tucked* is dialect) strings and swinging bells. In the first line of the sestet *justices* has a special theological sense: 'acts in a godly manner, lives fully energized by grace, justness, sancitity' (as explained by R.V. Schoder, S.J., in *Immortal Diamond*). In this way 'the just man' is 'being Christ'—as Hopkins put it in his spiritual note—just as, through the Incarnation, Christ expressed the perfect beauty attainable by all men.

Spelt from Sibyl's Leaves

Earnest, earthless, equal, attuneable,' vaulty, voluminous, . . .
    stupendous
Evening strains to be tíme's vást,' womb-of-all, home-of-all,
    hearse-of-all night.
Her fond yellow hornlight wound to the west,' her wild hollow
    hoarlight hung to the height
Waste; her earliest stars, earl-stars,' stárs principal, overbend us,
Fíre-féaturing heaven. For earth' her being has unbound, her
    dapple is at an end, as-
tray or aswarm, all throughther, in throngs;' self ín self steepèd
    and páshed—qúite
Disremembering, dismémbering' áll now. Heart, you round me
    right
With: Óur évening is over us; óur night' whélms, whélms, ánd
    will end us.
Only the beak-leaved boughs dragonish' damask the tool-
    smooth bleak light; black,
Ever so black on it. Óur tale, O óur oracle!' Lét life, wáned,
    ah lét life wind
Off hér once skéined stained véined varíety' upon, áll on twó
    spools; párt, pen, páck
Now her áll in twó flocks, twó folds—black, white;' right,
    wrong; reckon but, reck but, mind
But thése two; wáre of a wórld where bút these' twó tell, each
    off the óther; of a rack
Where, selfwrung, selfstrung, sheathe- and shelterless,' thóughts
    agaínst thoughts ín groans grínd.

Spelt from Sybil's Leaves is the first and much the longest of the self-
torturing sonnets Hopkins wrote in Dublin. Drafts of the first part
of it exist in his Dublin Note-book, in October and December 1884;
he reworked it and added to it during the following six months, in
which he composed his six 'terrible sonnets'. He did not send the
final version to Bridges until December 1886; but its mood is the
desolation of his first Dublin winter of 1884–85. However black its
subject, the poem shows Hopkins's poetic powers at their finest.
It is the only sonnet in which he uses an eight-stress line (marked
by a strong caesura after four stresses); the result, utterly appropriate
to its subject, is near a chant. He described it to Bridges as 'the longest
sonnet ever made', and wrote to him:

> Of this long sonnet above all remember what applies to all my
> verse, that it is, as living art should be, made for performance and
> that its performance is not reading with the eye but loud, leisurely,

poetical (not rhetorical) recitation, with long rests, long dwells on the rhyme and other marked syllables, and so on. This sonnet should be almost sung: it is most carefully timed in *tempo rubato* [irregular rhythm].

The title refers both to the prophetic books of the Cumaean Sybil, who guided Aeneas to the underworld (Virgil, *Aeneid*, VI), and to the *Dies Irae*, 'The Day of Wrath', from the Burial Mass: 'As David and the Sybil testify . . . what terror shall affright the soul when the Judge comes.' Paul Mariani has also shown the sonnet's closeness to several of Hopkins's Retreat notes for the meditation on Hell (*A Commentary on the Complete Poems* . . ., 1970, pp. 199 ff.).

The first half of the sonnet gives a haunting picture of evening becoming, *straining* to be, night: a darkness that, after the last rays of the dying sun ('Her fond yellow hornlight wound to the west'), swallows up all earth's variety and colour, the 'dappled things' Hopkins had celebrated in *Pied Beauty*. In this darkness, 'selving', distinctiveness, is all over. Hopkins's heart now warns him (*round*, archaic, is to whisper warningly) of the human analogue of this: *our* death will overwhelm us in the same way; leave us exposed to only diabolical shapes (like 'beakleaved boughs')—Mariani interprets them as our past evil deeds—in the blackness. This is the Sibylline prophecy.

The sonnet's final section, which applies the prophecy, seems to work on two levels. On the more immediately human one, it warns us that, if once life's multiplicity goes, and life is reduced to the 'black, white; right, wrong' of absolute moral judgment, we shall each of us be on a rack where, unprotected, we torture ourselves in endless self-conflict, as our thoughts grind against each other. But it can also be read as a warning of the Last Judgment. The reference in *párt, pen, páck* is to Christ coming to separate the sheep from the goats (Matthew xxv: 31–33); faced with this judgment, we shall suffer on the rack of our conscience—or, as Hopkins put it in a note on the Meditation on Hell, we shall suffer 'the worm of conscience, which is the mind gnawing and feeding on its own most miserable self'. On either level, it is a poem of dire warning.

Carrion Comfort

Not, I'll not, carrion comfort, Despair, not feast on thee;
Not untwist—slack they may be—these last strands of man
In me ór, most weary, cry *I can no more*. I can;
Can something, hope; wish day come, not choose not to be.

But ah, but O thou terrible, why wouldst thou rude on me
Thy wring-world right foot rock? lay a lionlimb against me?
    scan
With darksome devouring eyes my bruisèd bones? and fan,
O in turns of tempest, me heaped there; me frantic to avoid
    thee and flee?

Why? That my chaff might fly; my grain lie, sheer and clear.
Nay in all that toil, that coil, since (seems) I kissed the rod,
Hand rather, my heart lo! lapped strength, stole joy, would
    laught, chéer.
Cheer whom though? The hero whose heaven-handling flung
    me, fóot tród
Me? or me that fought him? O which one? is it each one?
    That night, that year
Of now done darkness I wretch lay wrestling with (my God!)
    my God.

Carrion Comfort is one of the six sonnets of desolation, the so called 'terrible sonnets', which Hopkins wrote in Dublin during the first eight months of 1885. On 1 September 1885 he wrote to Bridges: 'I shall shortly have some sonnets to send you, five or more. Four of these came like inspirations unbidden and against my will'; and, although he never in fact sent them, it seems certain that these were the sonnets he referred to. That May Hopkins had told Bridges: 'I have after long silence written two sonnets, which I am touching: if ever anything was written in blood one of these was.' Bridges suggested that *Carrion Comfort* was the sonnet 'written in blood'; but it seems more likely that Hopkins was referring to the even more desolate *No worst, there is none*, written on the same MS page as a revised version of this. In *No worst* there is no let-up; the poem begins and ends in despair. In *Carrion Comfort* Hopkins refuses to give in, to 'feast' on despair; he recognizes, in the final startled line, that it is God with whom he has been wrestling; and that, despite his frightened questioning, good will ultimately come from God's crushing him:

> Why? That my chaff might fly; my grain lie, sheer and clear.

There is a remarkable energy in the sonnet. It comes, of course, first from the images of physical struggle, of wrestling, to denote 'the war within'. The 'underthought' (Hopkins's own word for the unexpressed source of a poem's imagery) is clearly the Book of Genesis xxxii, Jacob's wrestling with God. But it comes also from the stressed transitive verbs and the packed, mostly monosyllabic, nouns and adjectives that go with them:

> why wouldst thou rude on me
> Thy wring-world right foot rock? lay a lionlimb against me?
> scan ...

(the stressed *rude*, used as an adverb, 'violently', exerts a particular force in the line). And energy is generated too by the repetitions in the first quatrain: six repetitions of *not* and three of *can* (all part of the rejection of despair).

In the second quatrain of the octet, the mysterious adversary becomes the winnower (subject of many of Christ's parables); then, in the sestet, the Master, whose rod and hand Hopkins has kissed. Line 11 adds 'joy ... laugh, chéer' to the hope of line 9. But, although there is light, it is still a 'terrible sonnet'. 'Cheer whom though?' The final three lines take us back to the wrestling and the agonized questions; and the sonnet ends with the bitter authenticity of all he has gone through:

> That night, that year
> Of now done darkness I wretch lay wrestling with (my God!)
> my God.

That Nature is a Heraclitean Fire and of the comfort of the Resurrection

> Cloud-puffball, torn tufts, tossed pillows ' flaunt forth, then
>   chevy on an air-
> built thoroughfare: heaven-roysterers, in gay-gangs ' they
>   throng; they glitter in marches.
> Down roughcast, down dazzling whitewash, ' wherever an elm
>   arches,
> Shivelights and shadowtackle in long ' lashes lace, lance, and
>   pair.
> Delightfully the bright wind boisterous ' ropes, wrestles, beats
>   earth bare
> Of yestertempest's creases; ' in pool and rut peel parches
> Squandering ooze to squeezed ' dough, crust, dust; stanches,
>   starches
> Squadroned masks and manmarks ' treadmire toil there
> Footfretted in it. Million-fuelèd, ' nature's bonfire burns on.
> But quench her bonniest, dearest ' to her, her clearest-selvèd
>   spark
> Man, how fast his firedint, ' his mark on mind, is gone!

Both are in an unfathomable, all is in an enormous dark
Drowned. O pity and indig ' nation! Manshape, that shone
Sheer off, disseveral, a star, ' death blots black out; nor mark
        Is any of him at all so stark
But vastness blurs and time ' beats level. Enough! the Resur-
    rection,
A heart's-clarion! Away grief's gasping, ' joyless days, dejection
        Across my foundering deck shone
A beacon, an eternal beam. ' Flesh fade, and mortal trash
Fall to the residuary worm; ' world's wildfire, leave but ash:
        In a flash, at a trumpet crash,
I am all at once what Christ is, ' since he was what I am, and
This Jack, joke, poor potsherd, ' patch, matchwood, immortal
    diamond,
        Is immortal diamond.

This is the third of the long sonnets, with codas (of, respectively, 20, 19 and 24 lines, as against the normal 14), that Hopkins wrote in Ireland, during the last two years of his life. *Tom's Garland* and *Harry Ploughman* were both written on holiday in Dromore, Northern Ireland in September 1887; *That Nature is a Heraclitean Fire* on 26 July 1888, on a day off from examining in Dublin, 'one windy bright day between floods', as he described it to Dixon. The experimenting with form in all three shows a new confidence in his creativity; the Greek thought that lies behind the first part of this sonnet reflects his lifelong interest in the Classics. But a letter Hopkins wrote to Bridges two months after writing the sonnet shows how much more he valued his own originality:

> Lately I sent you a sonnet, on the Heraclitean Fire, in which a great deal of early Greek philosophical thought was distilled; but the liquor of the distillation did not taste very Greek, did it? The effect of studying masterpieces is to make me admire and do otherwise. So it must be on every original artist to some degree, on me to a marked degree.

According to Heraclitus (*c.* 535–*c.* 475 BC) all nature is ultimately resolvable into fire. All is therefore in a state of flux: nothing escapes final destruction. The sonnet partly inspired by this philosophy divides into three parts. The opening section, lines 1–9, gives us an extraordinarily exuberant picture of racing clouds, light (*Shivelights and shadowtackle*, strips of light and shadow-patterns) and boisterous wind playing together; then, by a superb imaginative leap, they become the Heraclitean process: water, yesterday's floods, becomes earth, as the wind 'parches . . . stanches, starches' it; then all becomes fire: 'Million-fuelèd, nature's bonfire burns on.' But the wind has obliterated man's footmarks too, left by his toiling in the

Harry Ploughman

Hard as hurdle arms, with a broth of goldish flue
Breathed round; the rack of ribs; the scooped flank; lank
Rope-over thigh; knee-nave; and barrelled shank —
    Head and foot, shoulder and shank —
By a grey eye's heed steered well, one crew, fall to;
Stand at stress. Each limb's barrowy brawn, his thew
That onewhere curded, onewhere sucked or sank —
    Soared or sank —,
Though as a beechbole firm, finds his, as at a rollcall, rank
And features, in flesh, what deed he each must do —
    His sinew-service where do.
He leans to it, Harry bends, look. Back, elbow, and liquid waist
In him, all quail to the wallowing o' the plough. 'S cheek
crimsons; curls
Wag or crossbridle, in a wind lifted, windlaced —
    See his wind- lilylocks -laced —;
Churlsgrace too, child of Amansstrength, how it hangs or hurls
Them — broad in bluff hide his frowning feet lashed! raced
With, along them, cragiron under and cold furls —
    With a wet-sheen shot furls.

                        Dromore Sept. 1887

Hopkins's manuscript of Harry Ploughman

The Plough *by Frederick Walker. Hopkins
thought it 'a divine work', he told Dixon.*

mud (Hopkins has omitted the relative pronoun 'that' we would
expect between *manmarks* and *treadmire*); so that the second section,
lines 10–16, turns to the full implication of Heraclitus, that man,
both body and soul, will perish with everything else in nature. Three
characteristic word coinages express poignantly what would then
be lost: man's *firedint*, the fire given out by his being; his *manshape*,
'the very make and species of man' (as in the prose argument of
Henry Purcell); his *disseveral* being, his separate and unique selfhood.
The almost onomatopoeic force of 'vastness blurs and time' beats
level' is the crisis of this imagined destruction.

'Enough! the Resurrection' is the most dramatic *volta* (about-turn)
in Hopkins. The last two of the sonnet's three codas show how total
is the Resurrection's answer, in Hopkins's eyes, to Heraclitus. Both
'foundering deck' and 'beacon' look back to *The Wreck of the Deutschland*; 'at a trumpet crash' echoes 'as once at a crash Paul' of *The
Wreck*, stanza 10. The final coda is an impressive instance of Hopkins's
use of technical ingenuity to make crystal-clear the truth to which
the whole poem has moved: the bold and ingenious rhyme of 'I am,
and' and 'diamond', with the echoing of the short last line; the
alliterated vowels and consonants of the catalogue of man's inade-
quacies (seen as partly comic) before the Incarnation and the
Resurrection guarantee his ultimate value and permanence.

Part Three
Reference Section

Gazetteer

BALLIOL COLLEGE, OXFORD   Balliol began life in 1266 as a society of poor scholars, endowed by John Balliol of Barnard Castle, one of the most powerful of the Northern barons, as penance after a quarrel with the Bishop of Durham. Its foundation as a College was completed by John Balliol's widow Dervorguilla, in 1284. Founded ten years after Merton, it is the second oldest College of the University.

Many of Balliol's ancient buildings survived until the mid-nineteenth century. Then the College's expansion led inevitably to major changes. A new range in the garden quadrangle was built by Salvin in 1852–53; the early sixteenth-century chapel was rebuilt by Butterfield in 1856–57; and in 1867, Hopkins's final year, began the wholesale replacement by Waterhouse of the fifteenth-century southern front, facing Broad Street, the east side of the front quadrangle, the Hall and the Master's House.

Hopkins delighted in Balliol as it was when he came up in April 1863: it is, he wrote to his mother, 'the friendliest and snuggest of colleges, our inner quad is delicious and has a grove of fine trees and lawns where bowls are the order of the evening'. His first rooms were in the front quadrangle, in the roof, with at least the advantage of 'the best views in Balliol'; the more expensive set he moved into after a term were in Salvin's new range in the garden quadrangle, on the ground floor—or, rather, as he pointed out, 'four steps higher'—of what is now Staircase XVI. He liked both sitting-room and bedroom. Butterfield's new chapel he admired as 'graceful' and 'beautiful'—as he admired all of Butterfield's work he knew; its external colour bands of red and white, to which Jowett so objected, raised no complaint from him. It is difficult to believe that he approved of the demolition of the front of the college in 1867; certainly the rejection of Butterfield for Waterhouse, to replace it, did not help his feelings. Jowett, he recorded, 'held forth about proportion—after rejecting Butterfield'; and to his mother he wrote: 'There seems to be no conservative spirit at work at all in the buildings that are to be.'

There are very few references to Balliol or Balliol men in the letters Hopkins wrote when he returned to Oxford as a priest for ten months in 1878–79. But he saw a lot of Francis de Paravicini, now a Fellow of Balliol, and his wife; and he called on his old tutor, T.H. Green. To Baillie he wrote afterwards, when he had moved to near Manchester: 'Oxford was not to me a congenial field, fond as I am of it; I am far more at home with the Lancashire people.' Charged by Baillie with 'something of an affection . . . to run up the Lancashire people and run down "Oxonians" ', he first said that it may have been of 'Town', not 'Gown', that he was speaking; he followed this with something very revealing: 'I saw very little of the University. But I could not but feel how alien it was, how chilling, and deeply to be distrusted.' Some who had known him there before had been friendly,

> but with others I cd. not feel at home. With the Lancastrians it is the reverse; I felt as if [I] had been born to deal with them. Religion, you know, enters very deep; in reality it is the deepest impression I have in speaking to people, that they are or that they are not of my religion.

Just before this, he had made the comment already quoted (p. 16): 'Not to love my University would be to undo the very buttons of my being.' The conflict this reveals was only one of the many that the Victorian convert of Hopkins's strong feelings had to face.

BLUNT HOUSE, CROYDON   Dr John Simm Smith, Hopkins's maternal grandfather, rented Blunt House from 1847 to his death in 1877. It was a large mid-eighteenth-century brick-built house, with stone facings and a frontage of c.112 feet; its three-storey central bay flanked by single-storey wings; and containing fine carved woodwork. It stood on the southern edge of Croydon, to the east of the main Brighton Road. Its grounds may, in 1847, have extended to eighteen acres. They included a two-acre lawn behind the house, walled gardens, conservatory, plantations, melon ground, ice and summer houses, stables and outbuildings. During Dr Smith's tenancy much of the land was sold off (Hopkins refers to 'the cutting up' in his Journal, May 1868); at his death the house was sold with only just over two acres. Its trees, including two cedars of Lebanon and many beeches, were a particular delight to the Hopkins children.

HIGHGATE SCHOOL   The school was founded in April 1565 by Sir Roger Cholmeley, former Lord Chief Justice of England, as Sir Roger Cholmeley's Free Grammar School. The property with which he endowed it included two acres of Highgate Common and the old Highgate Chapel. Its transformation into a Victorian public school began under Hopkins's Headmaster, Dr John Bradley Dyne (1809–98), known within the school as the second Founder. There were nineteen boys when he became Headmaster in 1838, and 200 when he retired in 1873. Hopkins was there 1854–62, followed by his brother Cyril 1856–61. Hopkins just missed the great expansion of buildings during Dyne's headmastership: the 'School' and Library in 1866, the new Chapel (in whose crypt Coleridge had been buried) in 1867, two new boarding houses in addition to the existing two, Elgin House (where Hopkins was for a short time) and Berwick House. Dyne also added most of the present-day playing-fields.

Hopkins was one of the earlier boys to win an open award at Oxford or Cambridge. The school continued to grow and by the 1920s numbered *c.* 500.

MANRESA HOUSE, ROEHAMPTON This was formerly Roehampton Park, an eighteenth-century house built by the second Earl of Bessborough, in a village south-west of London, facing Richmond Park. The Jesuit Novitiate moved to it from Beaumont Lodge, Old Windsor, in 1861, and renamed it Manresa House, after the Spanish city, north of Barcelona, in which Ignatius Loyola wrote the *Spiritual Exercises*. Hopkins spent four periods here:

27 April to 7 May 1868, in a private retreat;
7 September 1868 to 8 September 1870, as a novice;
28 August 1873 to 27 August 1874, as teacher of 'Rhetoric';
1881 to 1882, as a tertian.

The house is a three-storey Palladian mansion; its west front has a fine six-pillared portico, flanked on each side by curving stone steps. The large grounds contained many trees which delighted Hopkins: cedars, Spanish oaks, elms and chestnuts. There were two serpentine landscaped walks, running round the north and south sides of the house, from the entrance drive to the lawn in front of the portico: renamed by the Jesuits St Aloysius' and St Stanislaus' walks. The huge walled garden was where Bridges took a peach and Hopkins would not let him buy it for him—as related in Bridges's *Testament of Beauty*, Pt IV. There was also a farm, farmed by the Jesuit community. Manresa House was badly bombed during the 1939–45 War. Most of the grounds have been developed by the London County Council and Manresa House itself is now a teachers' training college. The Jesuit Novitiate is now in Juniper Green, Edinburgh.

OAK HILL, HAMPSTEAD Gerard's birthplace, 87 The Grove, Stratford, Essex, was a three-storey semi-detached house (destroyed in 1941) in what was then a village on the eastern edge of London. In 1852, when Gerard was eight, the Hopkins family moved to Oak Hill, Hampstead (the house is now No. 9 Oak Hill Park)—a substantial house in a growingly fashionable district—and stayed there until 1886. Hampstead was then on the edge of the country; there are many references in Hopkins's Journal to the fine oaks for which Oak Hill was notable, to uncut fields, haymaking, and a variety of birds. It was popular among artists, writers and publishers. Keats had lived in Well Walk. The Hopkins's neighbours in Oak Hill included Leslie Stephen and, for several summers, Florence Nightingale; in 1912, still many years before Hopkins himself was known, J.J. Barratt, in *The Annals of Hampstead*, noted as living in Oak Hill 'Manley Hopkins, an authority on maritime law'. George Smith, the publisher, lived in Oak Hill Lodge from 1863 to 1872, and entertained weekly his *Cornhill* contributors, including Thac-keray, George Eliot, Mrs Gaskell, Trollope, and at least two painters whom Hopkins greatly admired, Millais and Leighton. In April 1868 Hopkins records going to a meeting of the flourishing Hampstead Conversazione Society (1846–72), founded to foster both the fine arts and 'a knowledge of scientific researches'. Besides his school poems, Hopkins must have finished or revised *Brothers* at the family home (it is dated 'Hampstead, August 1880'). He came here for a number of short holidays after he had become a Jesuit and his mother and father had become reconciled to his conversion. When his parents were about to move, he wrote to his mother: 'It seemed like death at first to leave Hampstead.'

THE ORATORY SCHOOL, EDGBASTON, BIRMINGHAM The Oratory School was founded by Newman in May 1859, the year after he resigned from the Rectorship of the Catholic University in Dublin and returned to the Oratory in Birmingham. It was intended to combine a religious education with a normal public school one. It remained small but, despite one crisis when several senior masters left, successful. Newman himself preached on Sundays and helped the boys to learn their parts in the Latin play—by Terence or Plautus—performed at the end of each school year.

Hopkins taught there, at Newman's invitation, for the Michaelmas Term 1867 and the Lent Term 1868. He was given the highest form, the fifth, with only five boys in it, and two private pupils to coach; but a long teaching week. He had already told Newman that he 'disliked schooling'; he complained to Baillie that he had no time and almost no energy and that he was anxious to get away from the place. The boys themselves he liked: of his own pupils he wrote: 'I feel as if they were all my children, a notion encouraged by their innocence and backwardness. They never swear beyond Con-found you, you young fool, and that only one of them.' The other masters too were 'nice souls', and he was delighted when his friend Challis joined the staff. He began to learn the violin and took part in the boys' football—being lamed by a kick on the ankle. The trouble was clearly tiredness (something that affected him more and more, as time went on) and a feeling of isolation: 'I put aside that one sees and hears nothing and nobody here'.

ST BEUNO'S COLLEGE, ASAPH, NORTH WALES The site for the Jesuit College of Theology, on a steep hillside, overlooking the Valley of the Clwyd, seven miles from the sea, was chosen by Fr Randall Lythgoe, English Provincial, in 1848; the architect was Joseph Hansom, the inventor of the cab. The Jesuit Theologians moved to it from Stonyhurst the following year. Hopkins studied theology here from August 1874 to September 1877; he was ordained priest in the chapel on 22 September 1877. He began *The Wreck of the*

Deutschland here in December 1875 and finished it early in 1876.

St Beuno's is neo-Gothic, picturesque, remote, and cold. Hopkins described it to his father the day after his arrival:

> It is built of limestone, decent outside, skimpin within, Gothic, like Lancing College done worse. The staircases, galleries, and bopeeps are inexpressible: it takes a fortnight to learn them. Pipes of affliction convey lukewarm water of affliction to some of the rooms, others more fortunate have fires. The garden is all heights, terraces, Excelsiors, misty mountain tops, seats up trees called Crows' Nests, flights of steps seemingly up to heaven lined with burning aspiration upon aspiration of scarlet geraniums: it is very pretty and airy but it gives you the impression that if you took a step farther you would find yourself somewhere on Plenlimmon, Conway Castle, or Salisbury Craig.

The legend of St Beuno and St Winefred (on whom he began a poetic drama) came to mean much to Hopkins. He described it to Bridges in April 1877:

> Who was St Beuno? Is he dead? Yes, he did that much 1200 years ago, if I mistake not. He was St Winefred's uncle and raised her to life when she died in defence of her chastity and at the same time he called out her famous spring, which fills me with devotion every time I see it and wd. fill anyone that has eyes with admiration, the flow of ἀγλαὸν ὕδωρ [holy water] is so lavish and so beautiful ... As for St Beuno he is a mythological centre to the Welsh and crystallises superstitions or till lately did, as for instance odd marks on cattle were called Beuno's marks.

STONYHURST COLLEGE AND ST MARY'S HALL, STONYHURST   Stonyhurst College, the Jesuit public school where Hopkins taught Classics for two years, 1882–84, is in the fell country of Lancashire, in the foothills of the Pennines, six miles north of Blackburn and four miles south-west of the market town of Clitheroe. It lies just south of Longridge Fell, with the Pendle range to the east, and is bordered by the river Ribble and its tributary the Hodder. The Seminary, St Mary's Hall, where Hopkins studied Philosophy for three years, 1870–73, is 300 yards west of the College, down what was then a quartz path.

Stonyhurst Hall, an Elizabethan mansion belonging to the Welds, a leading Catholic family, was given by Thomas Weld of Lulworth Castle, Dorset, to the English Jesuit Academy of Liège in 1794, when they were forced to flee after the French Revolution: the school's third migration since its foundation in St Omer, in North France, in 1592, by Fr Robert Persons, S.J. Professors and boys came by barge and boat, *via* Rotterdam and Hull, to Skipton, and the last twenty-five miles by carriage or foot. By that October the school was established, with forty boys, run on the same lines as at Liège. A Papal Brief gave 'the Gentlemen of Stonyhurst' (as they were known for the next thirty years) the privileges of a pontifical seminary; and throughout the suppression of the Jesuits (see p. 39) Stonyhurst was the centre of the ex-Jesuit and, finally, 'private' Jesuit world. New building began at once and continued throughout the nineteenth century.

It was still going on when Hopkins arrived in 1882 and wrote enthusiastically to Bridges about it:

> I wish I could show you this place. It is upon my word worth seeing. The new college, though there is no real beauty in the design, is nevertheless imposing and the furniture and fittings are a joy to see. There is always a stirring scene, contractors, builders, masons, bricklayers, carpenters, stonecutters and carvers, all on the spot; a traction engine twice a day fetches stone from a quarry on the fells; engines of all sorts send their gross and foulsmelling smoke all over us; cranes keep swinging; and so on. There are acres of flat roof which, when the air is not thick, as unhappily it mostly is, commands a noble view of this Lancashire landscape, Pendle Hill, Ribblesdale, the fells, and all round, bleakish but solemn and beautiful. There is a garden with a bowling green, walled in by massive yew hedges, a bowered yew-walk, two real Queen Ann summerhouses, observatories under government, orchards, vineries, greenhouses, workshops, a plunge-bath, fivescourts, a mill, a farm, a fine cricketfield besides a huge playground; then the old mansion, ponds, towers, quadrangles, fine cielings, chapels, a church, a fine library, museums, MSS illuminated and otherwise, coins, works of art; then two other dependent establishment[s], one a furlong, the other $\frac{3}{4}$ a mile off; the river Hodder with lovely fairyland views, especially at the bathingplace, the Ribble too, the Calder, Whalley with an abbey, Clitheroe with a castle, Ribchester with a strange old chapel and Roman remains; schoolboys and animation, philosophers and foppery (not to be taken too seriously) a jackdaw, a rookery, goldfish, a clough with waterfalls, fishing, grouse, an anemometer, a sunshine guage, a sundial, an icosihedron, statuary, magnetic instruments, a laboratory, gymnasium, ambulacrum, studio, fine engravings, Arundel chromos.

By then the school had 250 boys.

In 1870, the year that Hopkins arrived to study his Philosophy, St Mary's Hall was described as 'a plain, substantial building—a rather serious, studious-looking building—surrounded by trees, and quite out of reach of the "vulgar gaze".' By 1882, when Hopkins returned to Stonyhurst, two flanking wings had been added. In

1926 the Jesuit Seminary for philosophers moved to Heythrop College, Chipping Norton, Oxfordshire.

UNIVERSITY COLLEGE, DUBLIN   Hopkins spent the last five years of his life in Dublin, as Fellow of the Royal University and Professor of Greek of University College. Both were, in a sense, direct descendants of the Catholic University in Dublin Newman had founded thirty years earlier, in 1854. After many difficulties and conflicts of interest, Newman had resigned his Rectorship in 1858; the University had decayed; and in 1879 the English Government had established the Royal University of Ireland, mainly an examining body (as London University then was), in its place. University College was founded in 1882 as a constituent college of the new University, and the following year was handed over to the Jesuits.

University College, 85 and 86 Stephen's Green, in which Hopkins lived, had been Newman's original University buildings: they had fallen, Hopkins wrote to him, 'into a deep dilapidation. They were a sort of wreck or ruin.' The library had been removed, as the Jesuits came in, to a diocesan seminary. As a result, the College was, Hopkins wrote, 'for purposes of study very nearly naked'; the Catholic University's 'empty bird's nest'.

Hopkins is buried in Glasnevin cemetery, the graveyard of the Jesuit community in Dublin.

Short biographies

WILLIAM ADDIS, 1884–1917   William Edward Addis was a contemporary of Hopkins at Balliol and his most intimate Oxford friend. 'Of many letters some of them very long which Hopkins wrote to me I have not, alas! kept even one', he wrote to Fr Joseph Keating, S.J., in 1909. He was received into the Roman Catholic Church at St Mary of the Angels, Bayswater in October 1866, about a fortnight before Hopkins, and confirmed there by Cardinal Manning, together with Hopkins and Alexander Wood, on 4 November 1866. The son of a Free Church minister of Edinburgh, he was educated at Merchiston Castle School and Glasgow University and went up to Balliol as a Snell Exhibitioner in 1861, two years before Hopkins. Like Hopkins, he took first classes in Mods and Greats. He appears frequently in Hopkins's Diaries and Journal. Hopkins sent him two of his sonnets in 1865; they went on frequent walks together; and shared lodgings at 18 New Inn Hall Street in the Easter Term 1866. On a walking-tour together in June 1866 they visited the Benedictine Monastery at Belmont, Herefordshire.

Addis joined the London Oratory in 1868 and was ordained priest in 1872. He was a parish priest in Sydenham (where Hopkins once preached for him) 1878–88. In 1882 he was elected Fellow in Mental and Moral Philosophy, Royal University of Ireland (two years before Hopkins was appointed there); but resigned that October. In 1888 he left the Roman Catholic Church and married. Hopkins, greatly pained, wrote to Bridges: 'I feel the same deep affection for him as ever, but the respect is gone.' After two ministries, Addis became Professor at Manchester College, Oxford (Unitarian) in 1899; and Master of Addis Hall 1900–10. He returned to the Church of England in 1901 and finally became Vicar of All Saints, Ennismore Gardens, London, in 1910. He published several works on Church history, but is, ironically, best remembered by his *Catholic Dictionary* (with Thomas Arnold, Jnr), 1883.

ALEXANDER BAILLIE, 1843–1921   Alexander William Mowbray Baillie was an exact contemporary of Hopkins at Balliol and an intimate friend. The son of an Edinburgh doctor, he was educated at Edinburgh Academy and went up to Balliol as an Exhibitioner in 1863. He took first classes in Mods and Greats, joined the Inner Temple in 1866 and was called to the Bar in 1871. He practised as an equity draftsman and conveyancer at 5 New Square, Lincoln's Inn. He did not marry.

Baillie had a keenly rational mind and, although brought up a

Presbyterian, became an agnostic. He was described by the daughter of another Balliol friend as having 'almost a genius for friendship, being able to sympathize with and comprehend almost anything, while never moving from his own most definite roots'. He was thus a perfect foil to Hopkins, and they had a great affection for each other. Hopkins showed Baillie his early poems and his letters to him (published in full by Professor Abbott in 1938) begin with undergraduate zest: they are full of comments on painting and poetry and criticism and include the letter on 'Parnassian' already quoted.

In 1874 Baillie was threatened with consumption and went to Egypt; he returned cured. While there he pursued his interests in Egyptian archaeology and language. These chimed in with Hopkins's own later interest in Greek–Egyptian derivations. Letters (and postcards) flowed again; they met several times in the 1880s; and it was Baillie to whom Hopkins wrote his important letter of January 1883 on Greek tragic choruses, in which he put forward his theory of 'underthought' in the images of lyric poetry.

EDWARD BOND, 1844–1920   Edward Bond was a close friend of Hopkins at Oxford and accompanied him on his Swiss tour of July 1868. His father, who had a London furnishing business, moved from Manchester Square to Hampstead before 1862, and the friendship with Hopkins began there. Hopkins wrote to Bridges in 1866 that he knew him 'intimately'. 'He is handsome and very tall.' Bond was educated at Merchant Taylors' School, went up to St John's College, Oxford, as a scholar in 1862 and took first classes in Mods and Greats. He did not belong to any of the religious groups to which Hopkins belonged. As early as July or August 1864 Hopkins showed him some poems and was given great confidence, 'such as I never felt at all before'. In September he told Baillie that Bond was in fact a severer critic than Baillie himself, 'but he has not your great reticence, and blames and praises boldly, so that one knows what he means'. It was Bond's entreaties, apparently, that decided Hopkins to tell his parents he was about to be received into the Roman Catholic Church.

Bond taught for a short time at Radley and was in 1869 elected a Fellow of Queen's College, Oxford. He was called to the Bar by Lincoln's Inn in 1871. Bond visited Hopkins at Roehampton in 1872 and probably again in 1874; and in between Hopkins wrote to him about Matthew Arnold's poems and Newman's *Grammar of Assent*. But after that they seem to have lost touch with each other.

ROBERT BRIDGES, 1844–1930   Robert Seymour Bridges was the son of a Kentish landowner; his maternal grandfather was the Rev. Sir Robert Affleck, Bart. His father died when he was nine, leaving the family comfortably off. The following year his mother married the Rev. John Molesworth, Vicar of Rochdale, Lancashire. Bridges went to Eton, where he played in the Oppidans' wall and field elevens, was captain of his House, and strongly High Church in his religion. He went up to Corpus Christi College, Oxford, in October 1863, a term after Hopkins, took a second in Greats in 1867 and stroked the Corpus boat. He and Hopkins had become firm friends by 1865. After Oxford he travelled in Europe and the Middle East, studied medicine at St Bartholomew's Hospital and qualified in 1876. During his first job as a casualty physician (1877–79), he recorded that he saw 30,940 patients in one year. He was then assistant physician to the Great Ormond Street Children's Hospital; after a serious bout of pneumonia, he gave up medicine in 1881 (he had never planned it as a lifelong career).

Bridges published his first volume of poems in 1873, followed by *The Growth of Love*, twenty-four sonnets, in 1876. In 1882 he took his widowed mother to live at the Manor House, Yattendon, Berkshire; and two years later married Monica Waterhouse, eldest daughter of his neighbour, the 'Gothic' architect, Alfred Waterhouse. He lived there for the next twenty years; had a son and two daughters; and devoted himself to poetry, music, and his friendships. He edited *The Yattendon Hymnal*; published a long narrative poem, *Eros and Psyche*; and wrote important essays on Milton's blank verse (a subject Hopkins had been equally interested in). In 1907 he built himself a house on Boar's Hill, outside Oxford, where he lived until his death. He was made Poet Laureate in 1913; published his anthology, *The Spirit of Man*, in 1916; and his long poem, *The Testament of Beauty* (which went through fourteen editions or impressions in its first year) in 1929. The same year he was awarded the Order of Merit. He commemorated three of his closest friends, D.M. Dolben, R.W. Dixon and Henry Bradley, in Memoirs; and Hopkins in the first complete edition of Hopkins's poems, 1918. In his *Times* obituary Sir Henry Newbolt gave a graphic description of him as 'in presence ... one of the most remarkable figures of his time'; he referred to his 'great stature and fine proportions, leonine head', his 'extraordinary personal charm', and his character's 'greatness and its scarcely less memorable littlenesses'.

HENRY WILLIAM CHALLIS, 1841–1898   When Challis joined Hopkins at the Oratory School, Birmingham, in November 1867, having seceded to the Church of Rome in July 1866, Hopkins described him to E.H. Coleridge as 'a great swell and a friend of mine before the Flood'. The son of a Bank of England clerk, Challis was educated at Merchant Taylors' and went up to Merton as a Postmaster (scholar) in 1859. He read Mathematics and took a first class in Maths Mods and a second in Finals. William Bright regarded him in 1863 as one of the three 'chief mathematicians of the present year'. Though a close friend of Urquhart's and one of the High Church group, 'he never', Hopkins told Bridges, 'had much belief in the Church of England' and 'never used the same strictness in practices (such as fasting) as most of our acquaintance would'; Hopkins hoped that Challis's conversion would 'destroy his whimsies'. Hopkins was obviously very happy to see him at the Oratory.

Challis did not teach at the Oratory School long. He went to London and became joint editor of the *Westminster Review*; left the Catholic Church in March 1872; and was called to the Bar in 1876. He became a distinguished writer on the law of real property. In 1881, 'after many years' silence', he sent Hopkins an article he had just published in the *Contemporary Review*, which must have been of considerable interest to him: 'On Language as the Vehicle of Thought'.

ERNEST HARTLEY COLERIDGE, 1846–1920   Ernest Hartley Coleridge, grandson of S.T. Coleridge, and son of the Rev. Derwent Coleridge, first Principal of St Mark's College, Chelsea, was one of Hopkins's closest school-friends at Highgate. After Highgate he went to Sherborne School, then to Balliol in 1866. He read Mods and Greats, but, unlike most of Hopkins's Oxford friends, did not distinguish himself academically. He was a private tutor 1872–93, then devoted himself to editing the works of his grandfather and of Byron. He also published his own *Poems*, 1898.

In a long letter of 5 September 1862, beginning 'DEAR POET' and ending 'MIND YOU SEND ME SOME POETRY IN YOUR NEXT . . .', Hopkins sent Coleridge his poem *Il Mystica* and explained to him Tennyson's *Vision of Sin*; other early letters told him of the poems he was writing. Two other letters, of June 1864 and January 1866, show they had been discussing High Church doctrine. In October 1867 Coleridge wanted to visit Hopkins at the Oratory, Birmingham, and to hear Newman preach; but the visit probably did not come off. The following June Hopkins visited Coleridge's family at Hanwell, of which his father was now Rector. S.T. Coleridge's Note-books were then stored there and Humphry House suggested (in his *Coleridge*, 1953) that Hopkins may possibly have seen them on this visit. House pointed to certain likenesses in descriptive method and to the fact that both Coleridge in his Note-books and Hopkins in his Journal often use the sign /. There is no positive evidence that Hopkins saw the Note-books; but it is of interest that his first known use of the oblique stroke is in *Parmenides*, almost certainly of 1868, the same year as this visit.

VINCENT STUCKEY STRATTON COLES, 1845–1929   V.S.S. Coles was a close friend of Hopkins at Balliol. Only son of the Rector of Shepton Beauchamp, Somerset, he was a friend of Bridges and Dolben at Eton, and the recognized leader of the 'Puseyites'; 'prominent', wrote Bridges, 'for his precocious theological bent and devotion to *the cause*'. He went up to Balliol as an Exhibitioner in 1864, read Mods and Greats, but took only third classes. (Of his third in Mods, William Bright wrote to Canon Liddon: 'Of course one knows the effect it will have on the interests of the cause, in Balliol at any rate.') He became an intimate friend of Liddon and was Secretary of Liddon's High Church Essay Society, the Hexameron. Hopkins gave him his incomplete sonnet *To Oxford* in 1865. Coles did his best to mediate between Liddon and Bright and Hopkins, when Hopkins was on the brink of being received into the Roman Catholic Church.

Coles was ordained in 1869, succeeded his father as Rector of Shepton Beauchamp, and returned to Oxford in 1884. He was Principal of Pusey House 1897–1909, and one of the leading High Churchmen of his generation. He and Hopkins lost touch after Hopkins's conversion, but Hopkins met him again in Oxford in August 1879, when he told Bridges: 'I am truly fond of him . . . except these bonds.'

RICHARD WATSON DIXON, 1833–1900   Dixon's father, James Dixon, was a celebrated Wesleyan minister, as was his maternal grandfather, Richard Watson. Born in Islington, he spent most of his boyhood in Midland cities, where his father was on the Methodist circuit. He went to school as a day-boy to King Edward's, Birmingham, where his friends included Edward Burne-Jones and Crom Price (the first headmaster of *Westward Ho!*, Kipling's school), and where he won the school prize for verse with a long poem, *The Sicilian Vespers*. He went up to Pembroke College, Oxford, in October 1852 and was soon one of the leaders of a crusading 'Brotherhood', as they called themselves, which included Burne-Jones and William Morris, both at Exeter College. Like Hopkins a decade later, they particularly admired Ruskin and Christian art. After a third class in Greats, Dixon decided to become a painter and in 1857 joined Burne-Jones in London as a pupil of D.G. Rossetti. He helped to decorate the Oxford Union's new debating-hall with Arthurian frescoes, on which Hopkins later commented in his essay, 'On the Origin of Beauty'. (They later flaked and faded and had to be restored.) By the end of 1857 he had decided on ordination instead of art. He was ordained the following summer. After two London curacies, he taught at Highgate School (as remembered by Hopkins) for a few months from the end of 1861. He married the same year, and in 1862 was appointed second master of Carlyle High School. In 1868 he became a minor canon of Carlyle Cathedral; and in 1875 vicar of Hayton, a village seven miles east of Carlyle.

Dixon published the poems he had been writing since he was an undergraduate in two volumes: *Christ's Company*, 1861, and *Historical Odes*, 1863. In 1874 he began his monumental *History of the Church of England from the Abolition of the Roman Jurisdiction*; finally completed in 5 volumes in 1900. In 1882 he remarried and the following year published his long, early medieval epic poem, *Mano*, regarded by Hopkins as his greatest work. Two years later he stood as a candidate for the Professorship of Poetry at Oxford, but withdrew. From 1883 to his death he was Vicar of Warkworth, Northumberland; and the year before he died was given an Honorary D.D. by Oxford.

DIGBY MACKWORTH DOLBEN, 1848–1867 Digby Mackworth Dolben was the youngest son of William Harcourt Isham Mackworth and Frances, daughter of William Somerset Dolben, of Finedon Hall, Northants. His father added his wife's surname after his marriage and made Finedon Hall his home. Dolben was at Eton from January 1862 to December 1864, where he was an intimate friend of V.S.S. Coles and Robert Bridges, a distant cousin. His strong Catholic propensities got him into considerable trouble with the school; while still there, in 1864, he joined Father Ignatius Lyne's Anglican Order of St Benedict, and two years later was 'mobbed', according to Hopkins, on walking through Birmingham in his monk's habit and barefoot. As his photographs show, he had Hopkins's own slight build and delicate, refined features. He was singularly gifted and precocious. He wrote a great deal of verse while still at Eton, and six of his poems—of an unusual religious intensity—were published in the High Church *Union Review*, 1864–66.

In February 1865 Dolben visited Bridges at Oxford and met Hopkins. Although this was their only meeting, Hopkins was clearly strongly drawn to him. In his *Memoir* of Dolben, 1911, Bridges wrote: '[Dolben] must have been a good deal with him, for Gerard conceived a high admiration for him, and always spoke of him afterwards with great affection.' Hopkins and Dolben corresponded for at least a year after this meeting and exchanged poems. Their letters have not survived, but their copies of each other's poems have. The next six months Dolben spent in Lincolnshire, being prepared by a private tutor for Balliol. When he sat for matriculation, he fainted during the examination and was failed. In March 1867, after correspondence with Newman, he finally decided to become a Roman Catholic, much to his father's distress; he told Newman: 'Hopkins's conversion hastened the end.' He returned to his private tutor in Lincolnshire, without having been received, and on 28 June was drowned while swimming in the river Welland.

Hopkins was on holiday in France when this happened; his response to Bridges, on hearing the news, shows a characteristic mixture of candour and toughness—some of which reads almost harshly now:

> I looked forward to meeting Dolben and his being a Catholic more than to anything. At the same time from never having met him but once I find it difficult to realize his death or feel as if it

Digby Mackworth Dolben

were anything to me. You know there can very seldom have happened the loss of so much beauty (in body and mind and life) and the promise of still more as there has been in his case—seldom, I mean, in the whole world, for the conditions wd. not easily come together. At the same time he had gone on in a way wh. was wholly and unhappily irrational.

A further letter to Bridges, the same year, is even sharper: 'It is quite true, as you say, that there was a great want of strength in Dolben—more, of sense.' But Dolben's death and his own sense of loss must surely be the subject of a quatrain written in early 1868:

> Not kind! to freeze me with forecast,
> Dear grace and girder of mine and me.
> You to be gone and I lag last—
> Nor I nor heaven would have it be.

Over five years later, in September 1873, he recorded in his Journal, 'I received as I think a great mercy about Dolben': a phrase he uses elsewhere to express his conviction of a divine token signifying someone's salvation.

Bridges published Dolben's poems in 1911, with a Memoir (reprinted in *Three Friends*, 1932).

ALFRED WILLIAM GARRETT, 1844–1929   Garrett, W.A.C. Macfarlane and Hopkins were staying together in a Sussex farmhouse in July 1866 when Hopkins made his decision to become a Roman Catholic. Without having intended to, Hopkins told them both. Born and educated in Hobart, Tasmania, Garrett was probably the only Colonial Hopkins knew intimately. He came up to Balliol in 1863, took third classes in Mods and Greats, and became a member of the High Church Society, the Brotherhood of the Holy Trinity. He appears frequently in Hopkins's letters from 1866. Garrett joined the Catholic Church shortly after hearing of Hopkins's conversion, and stood as godfather (by proxy) when Hopkins was confirmed at St Mary of the Angels, Bayswater, on 4 November 1866. He was in the Indian Education Service 1868–84, when he returned to Tasmania and joined the Education Department in Hobart. He and Hopkins were still corresponding in 1882.

EDMUND MARTIN GELDART, 1844–85 Geldart's thinly-disguised autobiography, *A Son of Belial*, by 'Nitram Tradleg', in which Hopkins appears as Gerontius Manley, 'my ritualistic friend', has already been quoted (p. 17). Its author, son of a Nonconformist minister (his mother wrote children's religious books), had a strict evangelical upbringing. He was educated at Merchant Taylors' and Manchester Grammar School and went up to Balliol as a scholar in 1863. Hopkins gave his mother a vivid caricature of his appearance in his first letter to her from Balliol: 'His grey goggle eyes, scared suspicious look as though someone were about to hit him from behind, shuddering gait or shuffle, pinched face, in fact his full haggard hideousness'; but they became close friends, living on the same staircase in college. Hopkins was upset that Geldart took a second class in Mods, when he had clearly expected a first. In July 1865 Hopkins stayed with the Geldart family near Manchester.

On going down from Oxford, Geldart taught modern languages at Manchester Grammar School, then in Athens, and married a German. He was ordained in 1869; but in 1873 became a Unitarian and was minister of the Free Christian Church, Croydon, 1877–85. Early in 1885 'his opinions on many subjects were regarded as socialistic' by his congregation, and he resigned. On 10 April he disappeared from the Newhaven–Dieppe night boat and was never seen again. Hopkins, like others, supposed it was suicide, 'for he was a self-tormentor'. He had lost touch with him, but renewed his friendship some weeks before his death. Besides *A Son of Belial*, Geldart published sermons, books on modern Greek, and a translation of Zacher's *The Red International* (1885).

GEORGE GIBERNE, 1797–1876 George Giberne, Hopkins's uncle, was the son of Mark Giberne, a wine merchant. He joined the East India Company, became Judge in the Bombay Presidency, and on retirement married, in 1846, Maria Smith, younger sister of Mrs Hopkins. They lived in a Georgian house at Epsom and were frequently visited by the Hopkins family. Traditional stories of Hopkins as a boy in the Epsom garden, published by George Giberne's grandson, Lancelot de G. Sieveking, have already been given (p. 12). Giberne was a fine draughtsman, especially interested in architectural subjects, and an expert amateur photographer: Hopkins's early study of medieval architecture owed much to his uncle's photographs. Giberne's younger sister Maria Rosina was a close friend of Newman who, after her conversion, lived and painted in Rome and later became a nun in France.

ARTHUR HOPKINS, 1847–1930 Arthur Hopkins, Gerard's second younger brother, became a professional artist. He was educated at Lancing and studied at the Academy Schools and at Heatherley's. He worked for many years as an illustrator in black-and-white for the *Graphic, Illustrated News*, etc., much influenced by his friend du Maurier. He also contributed drawings to *Punch*. Forrest Reid, *Illustrators of the Sixties*, 1928, praises him as 'that accomplished illustrator ... a good draughtsman, with a strong dramatic sense, to which is added a sense of character'. Serial novels he illustrated include Wilkie Collins's *Haunted Hotel* and Hardy's *Return of the Native* (both 1878). Simultaneously he worked in watercolours, much influenced by Frederick Walker, whom Gerard especially admired, and in oils; RA exhibits (e.g. *Signals of Distress*) showed the family interest in danger at sea. 'My admiration in oil-painting was— and ever will be—Millais', he said in 1899. In 1878 Gerard wrote to Bridges: 'My brother's pictures, as you say, are careless and do not aim high. . . . But . . . he has somehow in painting his pictures, though nothing that the pictures express, a high and quite religious aim.' In 1888 he wrote a long letter to Arthur from Dublin, mainly criticizing one of his pictures, but showing a great interest in it, and asking for technical advice about his own drawing, which he had taken up again.

CATHERINE HOPKINS, 1821–1920 Catherine Hopkins, Gerard's mother, was the eldest child of John Simm Smith, MRCS, LSA, and Maria Hodges, daughter of Edward Hodges, a successful underwriter at Lloyd's during the Napoleonic War. Her father had been a medical student with Keats. She was brought up in 17 Trinity Square, Tower Hill, where her father practised as a doctor, and sent away to school at Brixton at eleven or less. She and her four sisters were all fond of music and great readers of Dickens. Before her marriage in 1843, she spent some time with a family in Hamburg and learnt some German. Four years after her marriage, her father, helped by the remarkable generosity of one of his women patients (which later led to a successful law-suit against her Will), moved to Blunt House, Croydon, a large country house. Catherine Hopkins valued Gerard's poems: *The Starlight Night*, one of the two sonnets he sent her in March 1877, hung, illuminated on parchment, in her house. A long series of Bridges's letters to her and her daughter Kate, 1889– 1919, shows the great interest she took in their publication.

LIONEL HOPKINS, 1854–1952 Lionel Hopkins, the fifth son of Manley and Kate Hopkins and the last survivor of the family, became a scholar of worldwide reputation for interpreting archaic Chinese scripts. He resembled his brother Gerard in looks and slight build and much loved and admired him. He was educated at Winchester and left as top of the senior division of Modern School. In March 1874 he joined the British Consular Service in China as a student interpreter; after serving in most of the Treaty Ports, he became Consul-General in Tientsin in 1901. He retired in 1908 on account of ill-health and lived, unmarried, in the family house at Haslemere, until his death, devoting himself to the study of Chinese scripts. His most important work was the collection and interpretation of incised oracle bones of *c.* 1300–1050 BC, on which he contributed numerous articles to the *Journal of the Royal Asiatic Society* between 1911 and 1949. He was a pioneer among Western scholars, wrote

Professor W. Perceval Yetts in a Memoir of him, in 'recognizing the importance of studying archaic Chinese writing as a basis for mastering the language'.

He shared a taste for puns and word-play with the family. An agnostic, he had no sympathy with the Jesuits. As a schoolboy he visited Gerard as a novice; Gerard, he said, to 'taste' his mind, asked him a lot of religious questions. 'Do you say your prayers?' was the first. 'No.' 'At least that's honest.' He could not see, he said, why Gerard could not have become 'an ordinary Catholic' like other people. Only one long letter from Gerard to Lionel has survived, written in March 1889 about Greek histories and philological works. The brothers regretted they did not meet or correspond more.

MANLEY HOPKINS, 1818–1897 Manley Hopkins, Gerard's father, was the eldest child of Martin Edward Hopkins, a London glass-seller, and Anne Manley, daughter of a yeoman-farmer, of Manley, Halberton, Devonshire. He was born in Dulwich, left school at fifteen or earlier, and *c.* 1833 became a pupil in a London average adjuster's office. In 1844 he founded his own firm of average adjusters, specializing in marine insurance, at 69 Cornhill, London; it grew into Manley Hopkins, Son & Cookes, still practising at 91 Grace-church Street. He became a leading member of the profession. On 8 August 1843 he married Kate Smith, eldest child of Dr John Simm Smith, at Chigwell. They settled at 87 The Grove, Stratford, Essex, where Gerard and three of the seven children who survived him were born. In 1852 they moved to Oak Hill, Hampstead, where they stayed for thirty-four years. In 1886 they settled in Haslemere, Surrey: first at Court's Hill Lodge, then at The Garth, which remained the family house till the death of Gerard's youngest brother, Lionel, in 1952.

Manley Hopkins had literary and musical interests and a passion for word-play, shared by Gerard and some of his other children. Throughout his life he wrote verses, sentimental, medieval, religious and humorous, of little creative power, but characteristically Victorian. He published three volumes of poems: *A Philosopher's Stone and other Poems* [dedicated to Thomas Hood], 1843; with his brother the Rev. Marsland Hopkins, *Pietas Metrica: Or, Nature Suggestive of God and Godliness*. By the Brothers Theophilus and Theophylact, 1849; and *Spicilegium Poeticum, A Gathering of Verses*, 1892. He also published three books on his profession, one of which, *A Handbook of Average*, 1857, became a classic on the subject. From 1856· to his death he was (initially through the influence of his brother Charles) Consul-General for Hawaii in London. His work was mainly commercial; but he also played a large part in establishing an Anglican bishop and mission in Honolulu; and in 1862 published *Hawaii: an historical account of the Sandwich Islands*. He reviewed poetry for *The Times* and wrote about twenty London newsletters for the *Polynesian*, the Hawaiian Government paper. On her visit to England in 1865, Queen Emma of Hawaii lunched with the Hopkinses in their home. Manley's last book was *The Cardinal Numbers*, 1887, to which Gerard contributed a letter. Earlier attempts to publish an essay on Longfellow and a novel were unsuccessful.

Both Manley Hopkins and his wife were devout High Anglicans. Manley was for a time churchwarden of St John's, Hampstead; for many years he helped to manage its funds and taught in its Sunday Schools. They were both, as was said earlier, shocked and distressed by Gerard's conversion to Roman Catholicism; but they became reconciled to his life as a Jesuit. The tone of Gerard's letters to them from 1868 on (mostly to his mother) is affectionate, if not very personal. It is ironical that, as Fr Alfred Thomas shows in his *Hopkins the Jesuit* (Appx 1), Manley describes the Roman Catholic mission in the first edition of his *Hawaii* much more attractively than he does the American Protestant missionaries.

WILLIAM ALEXANDER COMYN MACFARLANE, 1842–1917   The only son of a retired naval surgeon, of Edinburgh, W.A.C. Macfarlane had a Presbyterian upbringing. He was educated at the Royal High School, Edinburgh and Edinburgh University; went up to Balliol in 1863, but moved to St John's as a scholar the next year. He took a second class in Mods and, owing to illness, an *aegrotat* in Greats. He was an accomplished musician. He and Hopkins became close friends at Oxford as members of the High Church group. A letter shows Hopkins chaffing him, just before they stayed in Sussex together in July 1866, about his ritualist propensities. On 24 July, the day on which Hopkins told Macfarlane of his decision to become a Roman Catholic, Macfarlane recorded in his diary: 'Walked out with Hopkins and he confided to me his fixed intention of going over to Rome. I did not attempt to argue with him as his grounds did not admit of argument.' He had no leanings towards Rome himself and was ordained an Anglican priest in 1866. Hopkins invited him to visit him in Oxford in Spring 1867, but thereafter they lost touch. Macfarlane was Rector of Elmswell, Suffolk, 1878–91, when he succeeded to his uncle Alexander Grieve's estates and assumed the name of Grieve. In 1893 he relinquished his orders and retired to Impington Park near Cambridge.

BARON FRANCIS DE PARAVICINI, 1843–1920   Baron Francis de Paravicini, the eldest son of the Rev. Baron Francis de Paravicini, Rector of Avening, Gloucestershire, was a contemporary of Hopkins at Balliol, and lived on the next staircase to him in their second year. He came up as a scholar from Marlborough and, after a distinguished academic record (including the Hertford Scholarship in 1864),

became first a Senior Student of Christ Church and then a Fellow
and Tutor (1872–98) of Balliol, the only one of Hopkins's immediate
circle of friends to do so. His wife Frances was the sister of Robert
Williams, Fellow of Merton, one of Hopkins's tutors for Greats.
She was the author of *The Early History of Balliol College*, 1891 and
The Life of St Edmund of Abingdon, Archbishop of Canterbury, 1898. She
was a convert to Rome, and it was no doubt this that brought them
and Hopkins together when he returned to Oxford as a priest (at
St Aloysius's Church) for ten months in 1878–79. Hopkins saw a lot
of them and later wrote to de Paravicini: 'At Oxford, in my last
stay there, I was not happy, but there were many consolations and
none pleasanter than what came from you and your house.' The
Paravicinis, he told Bridges, were very kind and Frances de Paravicini
'a very sweet good creature'.

Hopkins met de Paravicini again in Dublin within two months
of his last illness. On his death, Frances de Paravicini wrote to
Mrs Hopkins:

> He was so lovable—so singularly gifted—&, in his saintliness,
> so apart from, & different to, all others. Only that his beautifully
> gentle & generous nature made him one with his friends; & led us
> to love and to value him. . . . in his religious life, he was *very happy*.

The de Paravicinis gave a font to St Aloysius's Church, Oxford,
in Hopkins's memory.

COVENTRY PATMORE, 1823–1896 Coventry Kersey Dighton Patmore
was the son of P.G. Patmore, writer and journalist, editor for thirteen
years of the *New Monthly Magazine*. He was educated at home,
published his first poems at twenty-one, and in 1846 joined the
printed book department of the British Museum. He knew Tennyson
and Ruskin well and contributed to the Pre-Raphaelite Brotherhood's
magazine, *The Germ*. In 1847 he married the daughter of a Congrega-
tionalist minister and had three sons and three daughters. His
best-known poem, *The Angel in the House*, 1862, the apotheosis of
married love, appeared first as four separate poems, published
1854–62. After the death of his wife in 1862, he became a Roman
Catholic. He remarried in 1864, retired from the British Museum,
and lived first in Uckfield, Sussex, then in The Mansion, Hastings.
The death of his second wife in 1880 left him financially independent.
When Hopkins met him in July 1883, he had recently married for
the third time. *The Angel in the House* had made him famous; *The
Unknown Eros*, 1877, his next collection of poems, passed virtually
unnoticed. In 1886 he published his *Collected Poems*, embodying a
great number of Hopkins's amendments; together with an Appendix
on English metrical law. During his last ten years he also frequently
contributed essays and reviews to the *St James's Gazette*.

Patmore made a strong impression on his contemporaries. 'His dominant characteristic', wrote Richard Garnett, 'was a rugged angularity, steeped in Rembrandt-like contrasts of light and gloom. Haughty, imperious, combative, sardonic'; but also, he went on, 'sensitive, susceptible, and capable of deep tenderness'. It was these last qualities that Hopkins undoubtedly brought out.

EDWARD WILLIAM URQUHART, 1839–1916   Although five years older than Hopkins and already curate of SS Philip and James, Urquhart was one of Hopkins's closest High Church friends at Oxford. Hopkins sent him two of his early poems for criticism—*Barnfloor and Winepress* and *A Voice from the World*, fragments of an answer to Christina Rossetti's *The Convent Threshold*; and he was the first friend whom Hopkins 'deliberately told' of his conversion.

The eldest son of an advocate and Sheriff of Wigtown, Scotland, Urquhart was educated at Edinburgh Academy and Glenalmond, and went up to Balliol in 1857. He took first classes in Law and History, tutored in both Schools for a time, and was ordained priest in 1863. After curacies in Oxford and Bovey Tracey, Devon (where he married, and where Hopkins stayed a week with him in August 1867), he was Vicar of King's Sutton, Northants, 1873–86, and licensed preacher in the Diocese of Exeter 1890–1908. At Oxford he was one of the leading High Church group: a member of both the Brotherhood of the Holy Trinity and the Hexameron. But he was clearly deeply perplexed about remaining in Anglican orders or joining the Roman Church. William Bright recorded in October 1865: 'Urquhart, last term, having read Ward's *Ideal*, told some undergraduates—much to their scandal—*that he thought Rome was right. To me, only the other day, he called the C. of E. "our poor dry branch"*.' Hopkins, in several letters, tried forcefully, even impatiently (as he confessed), but unsuccessfully, to persuade him to become a Roman Catholic. Urquhart published several polemical articles and pamphlets. According to his daughter, 'to the very end he spoke of the charm of Gerard Hopkins'.

ALEXANDER WOOD, 1845–1912   Hopkins met Wood early in 1864 through Alexander Baillie and saw a lot of him in Oxford: there are many references to him in his diaries and letters. He was received into the Roman Catholic Church on 15 October 1866, on hearing of Hopkins's conversion, and was confirmed by Manning with Hopkins and Addis on 4 November.

Wood was the son of a naval captain of Largo, Fifeshire. He had a strict Presbyterian upbringing; was educated at Harrow for two terms only, then by a private tutor; and went up to Trinity, Oxford, in 1863. He took his BA in 1870. After his conversion, he spent some time in Rome and America. He married in 1874; lived in

Sussex, where he knew Coventry Patmore; then in Hampstead. He published *The Ecclesiastical Antiquities of London and its Suburbs* in 1874 (Hopkins had originally been interested in seeing his 'beautiful architectural photographs'); and pamphlets in both English and Italian on Catholic questions of the day. He visited Hopkins after his operation in December 1872 and at Roehampton in March 1874, and sent him his pamphlet in favour of Catholics going to Oxford in 1883.

Further reading

Editions of Hopkins's writings

The authoritative edition of Hopkins's poems is *The Poems of Gerard Manley Hopkins*, 4th edn, ed. W.H. Gardner and N.H. Mackenzie, Oxford, 1967. It is based on the 1st edn, ed. Robert Bridges, 1918, and incorporates all known poems and fragments.

Hopkins's correspondence has been edited by C.C. Abbott in three volumes: *The Letters of G.M. Hopkins to Robert Bridges* and *The Correspondence of G.M. Hopkins and R.W. Dixon*, both Oxford, 1935; *Further Letters of G.M. Hopkins*, 2nd ed, Oxford, 1956. This contains his letters to his family and friends, and his correspondence with Coventry Patmore.

The Journals and Papers of G.M. Hopkins, ed. Humphry House and Graham Storey, Oxford, 1959, contains his diaries, journals, music, and a selection of his drawings.

The Sermons and Devotional Writings of G.M. Hopkins, ed. Christopher Devlin, S.J., Oxford, 1959, contains all his known spiritual writings, with Fr Devlin's valuable introductions.

Selections of Hopkins's poems and prose include *A Selection of Poems and Prose*, ed. W.H. Gardner, Penguin, 1953; *A Hopkins Reader*, ed. John Pick, Oxford, 1953; *Hopkins: Selections*, ed. Graham Storey, Oxford, 1967, and *Poems, by G.M. Hopkins*, ed. N.H. Mackenzie, Folio Society, 1974.

Bibliography

TOM DUNNE, *G.M. Hopkins: a comprehensive bibliography*, 1976, is the most up-to-date.

See also Kenyon Review *Symposium*, under Criticism below.

Biographies

The two most recent biographies are BERNARD BERGONZI, *G.M. Hopkins*, Macmillan, 1977; and PADDY KITCHEN, *G.M. Hopkins*, Hamish Hamilton, 1978, a more personal interpretation.

ALFRED THOMAS, s.J., *Hopkins the Jesuit, the years of training*, Oxford, 1969, treats his life as a Jesuit in detail.

All My Eyes See: the visual world of G.M. Hopkins, ed. R.K.R. THORNTON, Sunderland: Coelfrith Press, 1975, illustrates, with many reproductions of his own, his brothers' and his contemporaries' work, the visual aspect of Hopkins's life.

Commentaries on the Poems

DONALD MCCHESNEY, *A Hopkins commentary*, University of London, 1968.

PAUL MARIANI, *A commentary on the complete poems of G.M. Hopkins*, Cornell, 1969.

Criticism

Some of the best Hopkins criticism has appeared in collections:

KENYON REVIEW, *G.M. Hopkins: a critical symposium*, BURNS AND OATES, 1945, repr. 1975; includes a bibliography, and essays by Robert Lowell, Marshall McLuhan, and Harold Whitehall (on 'Sprung Rhythm'); (reprint includes essay by F.R. Leavis).

Immortal Diamond: studies in G.M. Hopkins, ed. NORMAN WEYAND, S.J., Sheed & Ward, 1949; a collection of essays by fellow-Jesuits.

Hopkins: a collection of critical essays, ed. G.H. HARTMAN, Englewood Cliffs, New Jersey, 1966 (Twentieth-Century Views); includes essays by F.R. Leavis, J. Hillis Miller and G.H Hartman.

G.M. Hopkins: Poems. A Casebook, ed. MARGARET BOTTRALL, Macmillan, 1975; includes essays by Geoffrey Grigson and Elisabeth Schneider.

Of many detailed critical studies of Hopkins, the following are particularly recommended (given in chronological order):

F.R. LEAVIS *in New Bearings in English Poetry*, Chatto & Windus, 1932 and 1950; a pioneering study.

JOHN PICK, *G.M. Hopkins: priest and poet*, Oxford, 1942.

W.H. GARDNER, *G.M. Hopkins*, 2 vols, Secker & Warburg, 1944 and 1949: the fullest study of Hopkins as a poet, if discursive.

GEOFFREY GRIGSON, *G.M. Hopkins* in 'Writers and their Work', British Council pamphlet, No. 59, London, 1955; particularly good on Hopkins's knowledge of nature.

HUMPHRY HOUSE in *All in Good Time*, Hart-Davis, 1955.

T.K. BENDER, *G.M. Hopkins: The Classical Background and Critical Reception of his Work*, Baltimore, 1966; makes a good case for his continuing use of classical forms in his poetry.

ELISABETH W. SCHNEIDER, *The Dragon in the Gate; studies in the poetry of G.M. Hopkins*, Berkeley, 1968.

PATRICIA M. BALL, *The Science of Aspects: the changing role of fact in the work of Coleridge, Ruskin and Hopkins*, Athlone Press, 1971.

R.K.R. THORNTON, *G.M. Hopkins: The poems*, Arnold, 1973 (Studies in English Literature, No. 53); a short and helpful introduction to the poems.

General index

Index to Hopkins's works

Acknowledgements

The author is indebted to *All My Eyes See: the visual world of G.M. Hopkins*, ed. R.K.R. Thornton, Sunderland: Coelfrith Press, 1975, both for the new light it throws on the visual aspect of Hopkins's work and for further facts about Hopkins's family, used in the family tree.

The author and publisher are grateful to the following for permission to reproduce photographs:
Bodleian Library, Oxford, page 15; Brantwood Trust Collection, page 22; British Library Newspaper Library, page 99; Cambridge University Library, page 83; City of Manchester Art Gallery, page 59; Leo Handley Derry (photo:Terry Williams), page 14; Bevis Hillyer, page 10 *top*; Humanities Research Center, University of Texas at Austin, page 10 *bottom*; National Library of Ireland, page 55; National Portrait Gallery, pages 9 and 85; Oxford University Press, pages 3, 41, 76 and 137; R.V. Schoder SJ, pages 49, 106 and 113; Society of Jesus (Bodleian Library), pages 13 and 121; Society of Jesus (Oxford University Press), pages ii and 51; Rector of Stonyhurst College, page 44; Tate Gallery, page 122.
The photograph of the kestrel from the Stonyhurst Collection reproduced on the cover is by courtesy of R.V. Schoder SJ.